Monetary Economics

Bank Notes

Series editor **David Palfreman**
Senior Lecturer
Central Manchester College

This series provides a structured revision programme for students taking their Institute of Bankers Stage 2 Banking Diploma examinations.

By answering a series of Short Answer Tests at the front of the book, students can decide on their revision priorities. Taking one topic at a time, they can refresh their knowledge of the topic using the Study Guide, and then test themselves using the Multiple Choice Questions. Most importantly, detailed notes on *all* answers to the Multiple Choice Questions are given, so that students can reinforce their learning by discovering why wrong answers *are* wrong.

Finally, by tackling the Post-tests for each topic, students can test the effectiveness of their revision.

There are eight titles in the series:

Law Relating to Banking
Monetary Economics
Accountancy
Investment
Nature of Management
Finance of International Trade
Practice of Banking 1
Practice of Banking 2

INSTITUTE OF BANKERS
STAGE 2 BANKING DIPLOMA

Monetary Economics

J BEARDSHAW

 Van Nostrand Reinhold (UK) Co. Ltd

First published in 1986 by
Van Nostrand Reinhold (UK) Co. Ltd
Molly Millars Lane, Wokingham, Berkshire,
England

Typeset in Ehrhardt 10 on 11½ point by
Columns Ltd, Reading

Printed and bound in Great Britain by
Billing & Sons Ltd, Worcester

ISBN 0 442 31754 9

Contents

Contents

Editor's Introduction

What's this book about?

This book will help you pass your Institute of Bankers examination.
Interested? Well, read on and you'll see how.

You're probably at the stage in your studies when you've got information coming out of your ears, a huge file of notes and the exam looming ever nearer! Quite possibly, you're beginning to get that familiar feeling of desperation: 'Where do I start?', 'I'll never learn all this.'

Help is at hand. If you use this book properly you'll discover where you should start and you'll learn more efficiently. Perhaps this will be the first time you'll have approached study in a methodical, effective fashion. By the way, we won't be throwing a whole lot of new information at you — you probably know quite enough already; there's nothing in this book which you shouldn't already know or, perhaps, knew once but have forgotten! Our aim is to help you understand, learn and use it.

So you want to pass the exam . . .

Well, your study should be: *positive*, *efficient*, and *effective*. Remember two *key ideas*:
— *Organization*
— *Activity*

Organization

Let's explain what we mean. *How well organized are you?* Do you waste time looking for things, do you spend as long getting ready to do something as actually doing it? How many times have we seen students ploughing through a thoroughly disorganized file to find something? What a waste of time! The point is made, we think; so get yourself organized.

Time: When are you going to study? Only you know when you've the time and only you know when you work best. For example, are you a 'lark' or an 'owl'? Be realistic. It's no good trying to revise for a few minutes here and there, while the adverts are on, for example. You must commit a *realistic* amount of time to any one session — probably not less than one hour and not more than three.

Have you ever thought of formally timetabling your study? Look at the timetable shown. You could draw similar ones (one for each week) and mark in your revision times.

As you can see, the timetable caters for both 'larks' and 'owls', as well as for all tendencies in between. Clearly there'll be major blocks of time when you can't do any study — you have to go to work — but that still leaves a lot of available time. Make the best use of it. A word of warning, however: if you have long-standing or important domestic or leisure commitments, think twice about breaking them. At least try first to build them into your timetable.

Study Timetable

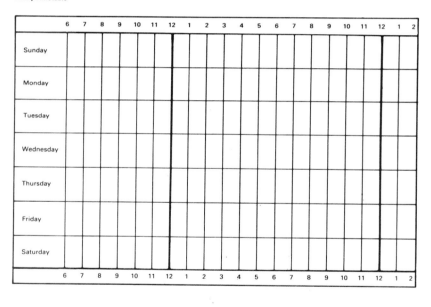

Place: The kitchen table or the sofa in front of the TV are *not* the ideal places to work. You need to be able to concentrate and this means finding somewhere *reasonably quiet* — don't try to revise with the Hi-Fi on! Equally important you need somewhere which is *comfortable*: a good chair, a desk or table, and good lighting. Ideally, you should be able to leave your work out, ready to come back to, so that you don't waste time at the start of your next session — one reason why the kitchen table isn't suitable.

Pace: Contrary to popular practice, it's *not* a good idea to leave revision to the last minute, particularly if you want to revise positively, efficiently and effectively.

Plan your revision: We've included some short answer tests which you should complete before reading the rest of the book. These exercises will help you identify your own strengths and weaknesses and so help you to determine how long you need to spend on each topic.

Use your study timetable to plan a revision campaign. Believe me, the more carefully you plan, the more you'll get done in any given time. Of course, you're bound to end up working like crazy for the few days immediately before the exam, so you might as well plan for this as well! What must not happen, and a planned revision campaign will prevent this, is finding that you haven't allocated your time properly and that there's just no way you're going to be able to study everything thoroughly in time.

Activity

How long can you concentrate on any one thing? If you're honest, not very long. And when it comes to revision, let's face it, it really takes the prize in the boredom stakes. No one likes to just sit there trying to learn something. But don't despair — there are ways to make it more bearable and effective. Read on.

What you should not do is sit there reading the same original notes over and over again. It's not only excruciatingly boring, it's also very unproductive. After you've read your notes through once, you'll find you know much of what you're reading already and progressively more of your time will be wasted each time you repeat the exercise.

Bank Notes: *Be active*, and this is where the *Bank Notes* series comes into its own. If you use each book properly (see *How to use this book* on p. xv) you'll find yourself very active in your study. In particular, you'll be interacting with the subject matter instead of being a passive, and not particularly absorbant, sponge.

Your aims: Remember, however, that this series is not a substitute for your own hard work; you'll still have to put in *time* and *effort*. Your study should have three aims:
 — Complete *understanding* of the topic.
 — *Retention* and *recall* of it.
 — The ability to *explain* and *apply* what you have learnt.

Study activities: So, a few general suggestions for *study activities*, all tried and tested, to achieve these aims. You'll find further ideas and guidance in the Study Guides to the Topics.

Revision notes: Your course notes and text books are not particularly suitable to revise from. Making revision notes is a good investment of your time. They can consist of just the headings in your notes/text book with, perhaps, a brief note about important principles or unusual points.

Do take care in the way you lay out your notes. Don't try to economize on paper; it's probably the lowest of your overheads anyway! Your notes should look 'attractive' and be easy to follow. Allow space to add other brief comments later. Try the following as a model:

MAIN HEADING
SUB-HEADING

....

Sub-sub-Heading

....

1. Important point..

....

2. Important point..

....

When you've made your revision notes, you can use them in the following way. Take each note in turn and try to recall and explain the subject matter. If you can, go on to the next; if you can't, look back to your notes/text book — perhaps noting a page number for future reference. By doing this, you'll revise, test your knowledge and generally spend your time productively by concentrating your revision on those aspects of the subject with which you're least familiar. In addition, you'll have an excellent last-minute revision aid.

Summary diagrams: These could be alternatives or additions to revision notes. Many people respond well to diagrammatic explanations and summaries; in particular, the visual association of the different aspects of a subject is useful.

We've two specific types of diagrams in mind: the 'family tree' type and the 'molecule' type, as you'll see below. Of course, if you've seen or can devise other types, use those as well.

Constructing diagrams is a particularly useful form of active study because you have to think how best to construct them and in so doing you'll find you better understand the subject. As with revision notes, don't include too much on each diagram and don't economise on paper. The impact and usefulness of a diagram depends very much on its visual simplicity.

You can use summary diagrams in much the same way as revision notes.

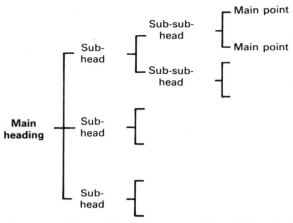

'Family tree' summary diagram (can be constructed vertically or horizontally, as here).

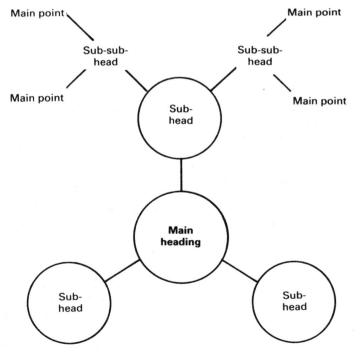

'Molecule' summary diagram.

Useful definitions and explanations: Each subject has a handful of points that are almost certain to come up in at least one question in the exam. So, why not prepare for them? (The *Study Guides* will suggest what these could be.) In practical terms, you may save yourself two or three minutes on each question simply because you don't have to think about how to define or explain something which you probably know well but cannot easily put into words there and then. Multiplied five times, those two or three minutes represent a considerable time saving. We've all wished for another 10–15 minutes in the exam before now!

Plan answers to past questions: Plan them, don't answer them fully. Once you've planned an answer, the writing out is largely a mechanical exercise. If, however, you feel you need the practice, answer some fully.

Examination technique

At this stage in your studies, there's not much we can say to give you a better answering technique. However, there are a number of general points you should remember about actual exam technique.

— *Read the instructions carefully*. You get no extra marks for answering an extra question and you automatically lose a proportion of the possible marks by answering too few. Also, answer the right number of questions from each section. Basic points perhaps, but you would not believe . . .

— *Read all the questions through* and provisionally select which questions to answer. Be careful in your choice; an apparently simple question may have a hidden twist — don't get caught. Similarly, in a multi-part question be sure you can answer all parts and not just the first.

— Everyone suffers from *exam nerves* and these will probably affect you for the first fifteen minutes or so. Consequently, it's often good practice to answer your 'best' question second or third. By that time you'll be thoroughly relaxed and working well.

— *Plan all your answers* — this is absolutely vital.

— *Divide your time more or less equally between questions*. There's no point spending an extra 15 minutes on your best question if it results in a very poor final question.

— *Check through your answers*. If you spend a few minutes doing this at the end of the exam, you can eliminate minor errors and give a final 'polish' to your answers. When allocating your time, allow five minutes for this.

What do I do now?

You may have been fortunate in your studies and have been taught some or all of the techniques outlined above. If you were, you should now be doubly persuaded of their effectiveness. If you weren't, you've already invested your time well because you're virtually guaranteed to perform better in the exam through having used them than you would otherwise have done.

Back to *Bank Notes*, and where they fit in. We've talked about being 'organized' and 'active' and we've given you a sound set of general ideas as a start. *Bank Notes* go further; not only do they provide an organized and active structure for study, they are also your *personal revision tutor*. Now turn to *How to use this Book* on page xv and start your revision campaign.

How to use this book

At any time in your revision campaign is the simple answer, but the earlier the better. Because we've designed the book to identify any weak areas you may have, and suggest positive ideas to help you study and revise, you'll find this book the ideal basis on which to plan that revision campaign. However, it's equally useful just before the exam when some self-assessment and new revision activities may well revive the flagging spirit!

The different sections

You'll find that this book has *five* sections:

— *Editor's Introduction*: a short but very important section which gives you tried and tested advice on how to revise positively, efficiently and effectively. If you haven't read it, go back and read it now and *only then continue with this section.*

— *How to use this Book*: the section you're reading now.

— *Short Answer Tests*: designed to help you identify your strengths and weaknesses in this subject.

— Ten *Topic Sections*: broadly following the order of the Institute's syllabus and containing:
   an overview of and advice on how best to revise each of the topics,
   Multiple choice questions and full explanatory answers designed both to test and to teach.

— *Post-tests*: designed to help you assess the effectiveness of your revision and identify any remaining weaknesses.

The short answer tests

You start with these; there's one test for each main section of the syllabus. Complete them all before you go on to the *Topic Sections*. Each test is scored out of 20 and we've allocated marks to the questions — usually two marks to each — and explained in the answers how to score. These tests will quickly give you a good idea of how much you know. By filling in the *Score Grid* — you'll find it inside the back cover — you'll be able to compare your knowledge and understanding on the different parts of the syllabus and identify your revision priorities.

Remember what we said about the value of organization? The *Score Grid* provides an effective chart on which not only to identify and order your revision priorities but also to plot the progress of your revision campaign and assess its efficiency. Look at the *Score Grid* now, and then turn back to here.

The topic sections

When you've completed all ten *Short Answer Tests*, filled in the *Score Grid* and determined the order of your revision, you can turn to the *Topic Sections*.

Study Guides: These, if you like, are your personal revision tutor. Each gives you an overview of the topic and a study framework. We indicate the points you really must know and be able to explain and use, and we point out common student mistakes and give advice on how best to tackle each topic. Some sections already contain revision notes and summary diagrams — remember the *Editor's Introduction* — and you can use these as guides for your further work. For example, if you're given a diagram which summarizes the entire topic, you could take each of the sub-sub-headings in that diagram, use them as main headings and produce more detailed diagrams on those particular parts of the topic.

You can also combine these introductions with the more general advice on study we've already given you. So, you should find that the *Study Guides* form the bases for very thorough revision campaigns on the topics.

Multiple-Choice Questions: You've probably answered 'MCQ' tests before. Such questions are an excellent way of testing knowledge and understanding but the feedback from the tutor is usually minimal, often non-existent. You don't usually know why your answer was right or wrong. Here's where the *Bank Notes* series is different.

It's through the MCQs that the books start to *work with you* to remedy your weaknesses in the different topics and reinforce the knowledge and understanding you already have.

For each question we've given you four possible answers; all are plausible and, indeed, all may be partially correct but only one is totally correct. After each question there's a space to put your answer — **a, b, c,** or **d**. You could also briefly write down the reason you chose that answer, just to stop yourself succumbing to the temptation of guessing!

When you've finished all the MCQs for a topic, turn to the

answers — they follow immediately — and mark your own answers.

You score two marks for each correct answer. (Keep a note of your score at the end of the test and enter it on the Score Grid.) We don't just tell you whether you're right or wrong in the answers — we give you a full explanation of why. You'll find these explanations very useful; quite probably the 'penny will drop' where it didn't before.

References to other books: At this point in your studies you might feel it's a bit late to start reading text books! You've probably had enough of them anyway. However, if you consider that you need to do some more reading on a particular point you'll find the books listed at the ends of the Study Guides useful. Sometimes we give you a specific reference but a quick look at a contents page or in an index will find you what you want.

The post-tests

The final section consists of 10 *post-tests*. These also use MCQs but this time you're just told which answer is correct.

You'll find that the post-tests largely retest what was covered in the main MCQs. This is deliberate. The purpose of the post-tests is to assess the progress you've made in your revision campaign.

You may like to answer them all together — a kind of mock exam if you like — and record your scores — *two* marks for each correct answer — on the Score Grid. You can then compare your score with those on the corresponding Short Answer Test and Main MCQ Test. While the comparisons won't be 'scientific', you will get a good indication of the effectiveness of your revision.

What do I do when I've finished?

If you work through this book properly and revise conscientiously following our guidance, you should be well prepared for the exam. However, if the post-tests reveal that you still have some areas of weakness you'll have to go back and revise these again — at least you'll know which ones they are and how to go about it!

Finally, remember our general advice on exam technique. The best of luck; we're sure you'll do well.

David Palfreman *Editor*

John Beardshaw *Author*

Short Answer Tests

Start your revision by attempting the
short answer tests on pages 2 to 7.

Questions

Topic 1   The concept of money

1   List the attributes and functions of money.   *(4 marks)*
2   Define Gresham's law.   *(2 marks)*
3   Explain whether or not a cheque may be regarded as money. *(2 marks)*
4   What is meant by **fiat** money?   *(2 marks)*
5   Give the main reasons for the introduction of the £1 coin. *(2 marks)*
6   Distinguish between money and liquidity.   *(2 marks)*
7   State the components of £M3.   *(2 marks)*
8   Which measure of the money stock or liquidity does *not* consist mainly of the liabilities of private sector financial intermediaries? *(1 mark)*
9   Suppose that on 1 January of year x the RPI stood at 360 whilst on 31 December of the same year it stood at 380. If a person had deposited £100 in a bank on January 1 what amount of money would they require on 31 December to maintain their spending power?   *(1 mark)*
10   Suppose that you have £1000 to invest. Over a 5-year period which of the following would yield the greatest return, assuming that the average rate of inflation over the 5 years is 8% pa, (a) an index-linked investment with a maturity bonus of 4%, or (b) a building society deposit yielding a net 9% pa?   *(2 marks)*

Answers on page 8

Topic 2   The UK financial system

1   What is meant by financial intermediation?   *(2 marks)*
2   List four non-bank financial intermediaries.   *(2 marks)*
3   Explain the process of maturity transformation.   *(2 marks)*
4   What is meant by 'the monetary sector'?   *(2 marks)*
5   Distinguish between primary and secondary banks.   *(2 marks)*
6   Define the term 'market loans' which appear in the clearing banks' balance sheet.   *(2 marks)*
7   Why is capital adequacy so important?   *(2 marks)*
8   Briefly explain why banks may make high profits in times of economic recession.   *(2 marks)*
9   Why are there so many overseas banks in London?   *(2 marks)*

10 What has been the main consequence of the Johnson Matthey affair (1984)? *(2 marks)*

Answers on page 9

Topic 3 Interest rates

1 Suppose that you borrow £1000 to help buy a car. This you agree to repay over a period of 1 year in 12 equal instalments of £100. Thus you have repaid £1200. Explain how you would determine the rate of interest you have paid for this loan. *(1 mark)*

2 Distinguish between the real (or flow of funds) theory of the rate of interest and the liquidity preference theory. *(4 marks)*

3 Why are long-term interest rates normally higher than short-term? *(2 marks)*

4 State three reasons why lenders may be willing to accept negative real interest rates. *(2 marks)*

5 List the reasons for high nominal rates of interest in recent years. *(2 marks)*

6 Explain how open market operations may be used to influence interest rates. *(3 marks)*

7 Describe four ways in which banks customers will be affected by a fall in interest rates. *(1 mark)*

8 What is meant by the 'term-structure of interest rates?' *(2 marks)*

9 Briefly explain what is meant by the interest elasticity of investment. *(2 marks)*

10 To what extent are interest rates internationally determined? *(1 mark)*

Answers on page 12

Topic 4 Monetary theory

1 What factors determine the demand for money in modern society? *(3 marks)*

2 Outline the theory of portfolio balance. *(2 marks)*

3 Consider the following information about a hypothetical economy: the money stock (M) = £30 million. The velocity of circulation (V) = 4; and the number of transactions (T) is 20 million per year.
  (a) What is the general price level (P)? *(1 mark)*
  (b) If the money stock were to increase to £40 million but the velocity of circulation (V) and the number of transactions (T)

3

were to remain constant, what would be the new price level (P)? *(1 mark)*

(c) If in the original situation the velocity of circulation were to rise to $V = 6$ and the number of transactions were to rise to $T = 25$ million, what would the new general level of prices be? *(1 mark)*

4 Comment on the following statement: 'If the GDP rises by 8.5% and the general price level by 4.75% while V is constant, then M must grow by 13.25%.' *(2 marks)*

5 What is the Cambridge equation. *(1 mark)*

6 List four effects of an increase in the money supply according to the monetarist school of thought. *(2 marks)*

7 Distinguish between the following:
$$MV \equiv PT$$
and
$$MV = PT \quad \textit{(2 marks)}$$

8 Outline the mechanism by which Keynes said increasing the money supply would lead to an increase in real GDP. *(2 marks)*

9 What is meant by the 'money illusion'? *(1 mark)*

10 Define the natural level of unemployment. *(2 marks)*

Answers on page 15

Topic 5   Monetary policy

1 List 6 weapons of monetary policy. *(3 marks)*

2 Identify the main effects of open market operations. *(3 marks)*

3 List the main points of the Monetary Control Provisions of 1981. *(2 marks)*

4 In what ways does monetary policy affect the exchange rate? *(2 marks)*

5 How do time lags hinder the operation of monetary policy? *(1 mark)*

6 Distinguish between qualitative control and quantitative controls on banks. *(2 marks)*

7 What is meant by the Medium Term Financial Strategy (MTFS)? *(1 mark)*

8 How does control over short-term interest rates affect the money supply? *(1 mark)*

9 Describe the operation of the 'corset' (Supplementary Special Deposits). *(2 marks)*

10   Evaluate the problems associated with using interest rates as a method of directing the economy in the long-term. *(3 marks)*

Answers on page 17

Topic 6   Balance of payments

1   Define the expressions **terms of trade** and **balance of trade**. Is there any relationship between the two? *(3 marks)*
2   What is meant by the term **foreign trade multiplier**? *(2 marks)*
3   Assume that a country is in balance of payments equilibrium on current account such that total current debits are £80,000 million and total credits are £80,000 million. If the combined elasticities of demand for exports and imports is 1.2 ($Ex + E_M = 1.2$) other things being equal, what would be the new balance on current account as a result of depreciation of 10% in the country's exchange rate? *(1 mark)*
4   List the possible cures for a balance of payments deficit on the current account. *(3 marks)*
5   In what ways will the choice of exchange rate regime (i.e. fixed, floating etc.) effect the possible policies to cure payments disequilibriums? *(2 marks)*
6   What effect do you consider a considerable rise in the price of oil might have upon the UK's balance of payments? *(2 marks)*
7   Why must the balance of payments always balance? *(2 marks)*
8   Consider the significance of the item interest profits and dividends to the UK's balance of payments. *(2 marks)*
9   What are sterling balances? *(1 mark)*
10   Briefly outline the difference between the Keynesian (or absorption) and monetarist approaches to the balance of payments. *(2 marks)*

Answers on page 22

Topic 7   Exchange rates

1   List four advantages of floating exchange rates. *(2 marks)*
2   What is meant by the bias of nationalism? *(1 mark)*
3   Under what circumstances would the supply curve of pounds in foreign exchange markets be vertical? *(2 marks)*
4   How do interest rates affect the exchange rate? *(3 marks)*
5   Does speculation increase or decrease fluctuations in exchange rates? *(3 marks)*

6   What is a 'crawling peg'?   *(1 mark)*
7   When Britain was on the full gold standard how would a balance of payments deficit be rectified?   *(2 marks)*
8   What is meant by the expression a 'dirty float'?   *(1 mark)*
9   Demonstrate graphically the effect on the US dollar of an increase in the demand for British exports to America.   *(2 marks)*
10 Does the theory of portfolio balance have any relevance for the determination of exchange rates? If so how does it work?   *(3 marks)*

Answers on page 25

Topic 8   International liquidity

1   What is meant by international liquidity?   *(2 marks)*
2   State two disadvantages of gold as a medium of foreign exchange.   *(2 marks)*
3   Why was America forced to leave the gold standard in 1971?   *(3 marks)*
4   The IMF Jamaica Conference took place in 1976. What were the main outcomes of this conference?   *(2 marks)*
5   Describe the main feature of the International Development Association (IDA).   *(1 mark)*
6   When was the OECD set up and what are its main functions?   *(2 marks)*
7   Rescheduling of international debts began with Poland in 1981. How are/might debts be rescheduled?   *(3 marks)*
8   The following is a list of official foreign *currency* reserves. Arrange them in the correct order, i.e. if you think most reserves are kept as dollar assets held in the USA then put this as number 1 and so on.   *(1 mark)*
    (i) ECUs
    (ii) Eurodollar deposits
    (iii) Other eurocurrency deposits
    (iv) Dollar assets held in the USA
    (v) Currencies other than US dollars
9   What are the main features of GATT (the General Agreement on Tariffs and Trade)?   *(2 marks)*
10 State two reasons for the international debt problems of less developed countries.   *(2 marks)*

Answers on page 28

Topic 9   Eurocurrency

1   Define a eurocurrency.   *(2 marks)*
2   State three major categories of depositors in the eurocurrency markets. I have done the first one for you. (i) European banks.   *(2 marks)*
3   List four centres of the eurocurrency market.   *(2 marks)*
4   What is meant by a roll-over-loan?   *(2 marks)*
5   In what way does the eurocurrency market affect the operation of domestic monetary policy?   *(3 marks)*
6   Name two institutions which attempt to monitor the eurocurrency markets.   *(2 marks)*
7   Why is it difficult for the central banks to control the eurocurrency markets?   *(2 marks)*
8   For what reason might a business prefer to hold its resources in eurocurrency deposits rather than the currency of its own country?   *(2 marks)*
9   Place the following categories of bank in order of importance in eurocurrency lending in London. If you think most lending was done by US banks in the UK place this first and so on.   *(1 mark)*
    (i) London clearing banks
    (ii) US banks in the UK
    (iii) Japanese banks in the UK
    (iv) Other overseas banks in the UK
10   Give two reasons for the growth of the eurocurrency market in the late 1960s/early 1970s.   *(2 marks)*

Answers on page 31

Answers

Topic 1   The concept of money

1 **Functions**
1 Medium of exchange
2 Unit of account
3 Store of value
4 Standard of deferred payment

Attributes
1 Acceptability
2 Durability
3 Homogeneity
4 Divisibility
5 Portability
6 Stability of value
7 Difficult to counterfeit.

(Score ½ a mark for each correct answer in list A; ½ a mark for each two correct answers in List B.)

/4

2 'Bad money drives out good'. Named after Sir Thomas Gresham (1519–79) a leading Elizabethan businessman and founder of the Royal Exchange. If two coins are in circulation where nominal values are the same but whose bullion contents differ, the 'dearer' one will be withdrawn and melted down.

/2

3 No! It is the bank deposit which the cheque accesses that is the money. If this distinction did not exist a bank could discharge its responsibility to its depositors by giving them a cheque drawn on themselves. Nonetheless, much of our money supply could colloquially be termed 'cheque-money'.

/2

4 Money which is decreed by law (*fiat*) to be acceptable in settlement of debts. Thus, *legal tender* is *fiat* money. However, the term is more usually applied when money is only legally acceptable but has generally become unusable, eg. the German mark 1945–47.

/2

5 The pound note has been falling down on the durability attribute. Also inflation has led to an increased demand for a higher denomination coin for use in slot-machines. (Score 1 mark for each reason)

/2

6 Confusion may arise because money is the most liquid asset. However, liquidity refers to the ease with which an asset may be turned into money

(liquified). Liquid assets consist of such things as Treasury bills and certificates of deposit, which can be turned into cash without loss.

7 See Figure A.1.

/2

8 M0, the wide money base. This consists mainly of notes and coins which are liabilities of the public sector. All other definitions consist mainly of deposits (liabilities) of financial intermediaries.

/1

9 $\dfrac{380}{360} \times £100 = £105.56$

/1

10 (a) Maturity value of principal

$£1000 \times (1.08)^5$ = $£1,469.33$
Plus bonus (4%)   58.77

                                   $£1,528.10$

(b) Value of investment after 5 years
$£1000 \times (1.09)^5$ = $£1,538.62$
Thus the correct answer is (b).

/2

your total score for this Topic . . . . /20

Topic 2   The UK financial system

1 Financial intermediation is the process by which institutions act to channel funds from surplus units to deficit units in the community, thereby standing between the ultimate lenders and ultimate borrowers in society. For example, the saver (ultimate lender) places money on deposit with a bank which then lends out to another customer (ultimate borrower), thereby acting as an intermediary or go-between.

/2

2 Building societies, finance houses, pension funds and insurance companies. (Score ½ a mark for each correct answer)

/2

3 To summarize the process of maturity transformation we could say that banks etc. 'borrow short and lend long'. That is to say they accept deposits from customers which may, for example, be held on current account in which case they are highly liquid whilst most of this money is then lent out for a longer period of time to customers. This therefore

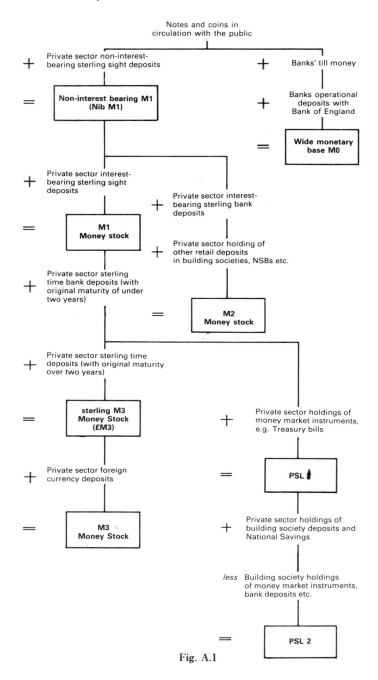

Fig. A.1

satisfies the borrower's need for longer-term finance and the lender's need for liquidity. Whilst this operation is very uncertain on an individual basis, banks accomplish it by pooling together thousands of such transactions; thereby transforming and reducing the risk.

/2

4 The 'monetary sector' is the group of financial institutions (banks and LDTs) subject to the immediate supervision of the Bank of England. It is defined by the 1981 Monetary Control – Provisions and replaces the previous 'banking sector'. For a fuller explanation see the Study Guide on page 46.

/2

5 Primary banks are concerned with the money transmission mechanism whereas secondary banks e.g. the Accepting Houses are usually concerned mainly with dealing with other financial intermediaries.

/2

6 The market referred to is the money market. Market loans are loans made in this market for short-periods of time ranging from overnight to 3 months. Money lent 'at call' to discount houses and inter-bank loans would be examples of such loans.

/2

7 Capital adequacy means that a bank should have a suitable and acceptable asset structure. This is obviously vitally important since it relates to the bank's ability to meet its obligations. What is suitable will depend upon the type of deposits it has accepted and the type of loans it has made. The consequences of having badly structured assets can be seen from the secondary banking crisis of 1973 and the failure of Johnson Matthey (1984).

/2

8 It does not follow that banks will automatically make high profits in times of recession. The failure of thousands of USA banks in the 1930s is evidence of this. However, in recent years the very high real interest rates which have accompanied the recession have led to high profits for the banks. On the other hand risk is increased because of the increased possibility of bad debts.

/2

9 As a centre of world trade and commerce, London has always attracted foreign banks. In recent years

their growth has been accelerated by the need to serve the European needs of their customers back at home. They have also been attracted by the Eurocurrency market. They have now begun to compete with British banks in domestic markets, e.g. in the provision of corporate loans.

/2

10 Briefly the government and the Bank of England have brought in much tighter supervision of the monetary sector. It will probably also lead to the abolition of the distinction between banks and LDTs.

/2

your total score for this Topic . . . . /20

Topic 3 Interest rates

1 The question is designed to draw your attention to the effect a diminishing balance has upon the rates of interest. Thus if you repay £100 after the first month then you have only borrowed the full £1000 for 1 month. After this the amount you owe is less and decreases each successive month. Therefore if you repay £200 in addition to the £1000 borrowed you have paid a rate of interest well in excess of the 20% which the simple interest calculation would suggest.

There is no simple way to calculate the correct answer. Usually it is arrived at by looking it up in the tables published by finance houses and the like. In fact in this case the true rate of interest is 23.4%.

/1

2 The answer to this question could quite easily fill a large book. The essential points should include the following: the real (flow funds or loanable funds) theory is the classical theory of rate interest. It is also the basis of the more modern monetarist theory. It is termed real because it is believed that the rate of interest is ultimately determined by the real net productivity of capital. The theory assumes that the demand and supply of funds is kept in equilibrium by the rate of interest.

The liquidity preference theory is based on the work of Keynes. He put forward several motives for holding money – transactions, precautionary and speculative. Because of the speculative motive

Keynes believed that people may from time to time wish to hold money as an asset. This gives rise to the liquidity preference schedule for money where the demand for money is inversely proportional to the rate of interest. Keynes' theory is notorious, however, for failing to explain what determines the supply of money.

Your score

/4

3   Long-term interest rates are usually higher because of the greater risk and uncertainty involved in parting with money for a longer period of time. In addition to this the Keynesian point of view would maintain that people need encouragement (i.e. higher interest rates) to compensate for the inconvenience of foregoing liquidity for a longer period of time.

/2

4   (a) The main reasons for personal savings are not connected with the rate of interest. Thus some saving will take place whatever the rate.
    (b) Institutions such as banks who have to lend money to exist may be forced to accept negative rates.
    (c) Investors may expect that the rate of inflation may fall.
    (Score 1 mark for 2 correct answers, 2 marks for all 3)

/2

5   (a) High rates of inflation.
    (b) Increased uncertainty.
    (c) Heavy government borrowing.
    (d). Restrictive monetary policies.
    (e) High rates overseas especially the USA.
    (Score 1 mark for 2 correct answers, 2 marks for 5 correct answers)

/2

6   Interest rates may be affected as the government has to increase interest rates to encourage extra purchases of bills or bonds, or conversely, interest rates may decrease if the government restricts open market sales. Extra sales depress the price of securities thus raising interest rates, while restricting sales force up the price of securities and thereby depress the rate of interest. However, the greatest effect is likely to come from the secondary effects as banks have to adjust their balance sheets as a result of open market operations. Open market sales to the non-bank

private sector, for example, should bring about a multiple contraction of banks' assets causing them to restrict lending and sell-off securities both of which will increase the rate of interest. This process would be reversed in the event of open market purchases.

/3

7   (a) Lower rate of interest on deposits
    (b) Cost of borrowing decreases
    (c) Customers with non-interest bearing accounts may find their bank charges increased
    (d) Corporate customers may find their profitability increased.

/1

8   The term-structure of interest rates means that interest rates on a loan tend to be related to the term of the loan, very short-term loans normally having lower rates than long-term ones. However, the rate may also be affected by such things as expectations of the future rates of inflation and the future rate of interest. (It is also possible for very short-term rates, e.g. overnight, to be extremely high for brief periods.)

/2

9   The interest elasticity of investment refers to the extent to which investment is affected by changes in the rate of interest. If investment is greatly affected by changes in the rate of interest then it is said to be interest elastic, whereas if interest rate changes do not greatly affect the rate of investment it is said to be interest inelastic. The degree of elasticity will be affected by whether we are considering changes at a high or low rate of interest q.v. normal rules of elasticity.

There is disagreement between Keynesians and monetarists on this topic. Do not confuse this with the controversy surrounding the liquidity trap which is concerned with changes in the money stock, not with changes in the interest rate.

/2

10 Interest rates are significantly affected by international influences. This is especially so for a nation like the UK which is an international centre for banking and finance. It becomes increasingly difficult for us to follow an independent policy on interest rates. This is well evidenced by the effect of high US interest rates in the mid 1980s. A country with strict

Your score

exchange control, such as France, may find it easier to isolate itself from international influences.

your total score for this Topic . . . . /20

Topic 4   Monetary theory

1   This is a contentious issue. Keynesians would say there are three factors: the transactions, precautionary, and speculative motives but monetarists would only agree with the first of these. These factors are in turn influenced by the level of income and by the rate of interest. (Score 1 mark for transactions and precautionary motive, 1 for speculative and 1 for mentioning other factors)

/3

2   Portfolio balance refers to the way in which people distribute their wealth between various assets. Friedman says that there are five main categories of wealth:
(a) money
(b) bonds
(c) equities
(d) physical goods
(e) human wealth
People try to obtain the most desirable distribution of their wealth between these assets to gain interest, for convenience etc. There is disagreement between the schools of thought, monetarists believing that money is a substitute for all other assets, while Keynesians believe that money is a close substitute only for financial assets such as bonds. (Score 1 mark for listing assets and 1 for exploring differences between monetarist and Keynesian views)

/2

3   (a) £6
(b) £8 = an increase of 33.3%
(c) £7.20 = an increase of 20%
(Score 1 mark for each correct answer)

/3

4   If real GDP rose by 8.5% and V were constant then M would rise by something like 13.25%. However, these constants are not stated in the question, it is therefore possible that V might change making it impossible to come to such a definite conclusion. We are concerned here with one of the central arguments

of monetary economics, i.e. the relationship between changes in M and inflation. Thus, some uncertainty in your answer can be excused! (Score 1 mark for appreciating assumptions and 1 mark for exploring disagreements)

Your score

/2

5   The Cambridge equation is a reformulation of the quantity equation; it is:
    M = Kpr
    Where **M** is the quantity of money, **K** is the liquidity proportion (the fraction of income held in cash), **p** is the price level and **r** is the real national income (the amount of goods and services produced).

/1

6   (a) Prices will rise if the economy is at full employment
    (b) Interest rates will fall in the short-run
    (c) People will spend more on other assets such as bonds and real physical assets (not just bonds as Keynes suggested)
    (d) There may be a rise in real incomes in the short-run but in the long-run the increased money supply will only affect prices not output. (Score 1 mark for each two correct answers, no half marks!)

/2

7   The first expression is an identity while the second is an equation, i.e. the first says that the money stock (M) multiplied by the velocity of circulation (V) is the *same thing* as the value of national income ($P \times T$). However, if we make assumptions about the behaviour of some of the components, the expression then becomes an equation. Monetarists (great simplification) believe that V and T are constants. Thus, we have a formula which predicts the effects of changes in the money supply on the price level. (Score 1 mark each for explaining the assumptions of each equation)

/2

8   Keynes argued that increasing the money stock would lower the rate of interest and this in turn would increase investment and thereby the level of real national income. He believed, however, that this was a fairly weak connection and that GDP would be better stimulated by a budget deficit. (Score 1 mark

for explaining the mechanism and 1 mark for appreciating that it is weak and Keynes preferred fiscal measures)

Your score

/2

9 'Money illusion' refers to the fact that inflation may fool people into thinking that they are better off as their money income increases. The monetarist school maintains that this illusion may persist for some time but people eventually realize that inflation has taken the real rise in income away from them. The new 'rational expectations' school maintains that people are not deceived by purely monetary changes.

/1

10 Both the monetarists and rational expectations schools of thought believe that there is a natural level of unemployment. Employment may be pushed above this level by government policies such as budget deficits but this will be inflationary. It is also held that it may be necessary to depress the level of employment below the natural level in order to eliminate inflation. However, in the long-run the economy must settle at the natural level of unemployment. It has proved impossible however, to say precisely what this level is. (Score 1 mark for exploring the idea and 1 mark for appreciating its significance in the Phillips curve).

/2

your total score for this Topic . . . . /20

Topic 5 Monetary policy

1 Open market operations
Special deposits
Special directives
Funding
Moral suasion
Liquidity ratios
(Score 1 mark for each 2 correct answers, no ½ marks)

/3

2 These are fully described in the study guide (p.97). (Score 1 mark for knowing the effect of purchases and sales and the remaining 2 marks for describing how they affect the banks' balance sheets)

/3

3 (a) Each institution in the monetary sector was required to keep 0.5% of its eligible liabilities in

17

Your score

a non-operational account at the Bank of England.

(b) A new 'monetary sector', somewhat broader than the old 'banking sector', was defined. It included:
   * All recognized banks and LDTs
   * National Girobank
   * Those banks in the Channel Islands and Isle of Man which comply with the Bank's regulations
   * Trustee Savings Banks (TSBs)
   * The Banking Department of the Bank of England

(c) Eligible liabilities were to be calculated in an integrated uniform manner for all institutions.

(d) The special deposit scheme was retained.

(e) The list of institutions whose acceptance (of bills of exchange) were eligible for discount at the Bank was widened.

(f) The reserve assets ratio was abolished.

(g) The Bank of England discontinued the regular 'posting' of the minimum lending rate (MLR). Instead the Bank now operates within an unstated band of interest rates. However, it retains the right to announce the rate at which it will operate if it thinks necessary.

(To score 1 mark you must have points (a) and (b). Then give yourself a further mark for any 4 other correct points)

/2

4 In a country such as the UK which is both very dependent on international trade and a major world banking sector, exchange rates are extremely important. The exchange rate is affected by interest rates and the resultant effect upon capital flows. Raising interest rates tends to attract overseas investment thus raising the exchange rate and vice versa. Overseas confidence in the currency will also be affected by the performance of major indicators such as the RPI and M3. In the long term the success (or otherwise) of monetary policy in promoting the well-being of the economy will, of course, fundamentally affect exchange rates. The level of inflation, in particular, has a direct effect on the exchange rate through purchasing power parity.

(Score 1 mark for stating how interest rates affect flows of currency and 1 mark for the influence of monetary policy on economic performance)

5   Time lags are a major problem with monetary policy (and other forms of policy). That is to say, delays may mean that policies cease to be appropriate. It is possible to recognize three types of lags:

(a) The recognition lag refers to the time it takes for a government to recognize a problem. For example, are a bad quarter's figures for the balance of payments just a fluke or the start of a major downward trend? The government must decide.

(b) The implementation lag is concerned with the time after recognition which it takes for a government to decide on and implement a policy, e.g. a rise in interest rates.

(c) The operation lag. After implementation it will take some time for the policy to have an effect in the economy. For example, Friedman argued that changes in the price level lagged $1\frac{1}{2}$–2 years behind changes in the money stock. (Score 1 mark for correctly identifying the reasons. Well done if you got all three)

/1

6   Direct controls upon the banking system can be divided into quantitative and qualitative. Quantitative controls include special deposits, the 'corset' and, the now abandoned, quantitative special directives. Qualitative controls are those attempting to influence the types of bank lending.

It can, of course, be argued that other indirect weapons of policy such as open market operations are quantitative. (Score 1 mark for correctly describing each type of control)

/2

7   The Medium Term Financial Strategy was first introduced in 1980. This set publicly announced targets for the growth of the money supply for the 3–4 years ahead. It set targets for such things as the size of PSBR, the growth of £M3 etc. The aim was that by setting progressively lower targets for these figures, expectations of inflation would be reduced. MTFS is in line with the thinking of the rational

expectation school of economics (see p.82). (Score 1 mark for each definition — see Study Guide)

Your score /1

8 The straightforward answer is that raising interest rates should restrict the money supply by making it more expensive to borrow. However, in the short term higher interest rates are unlikely to deter private sector borrowing. It is even possible that raising the interest rate will *increase* the money stock by:

* attracting overseas investment in sterling
* increasing 'distress' borrowing by companies

(To score your mark, you must make both the contradictory and expansionary points)

/1

9 The Special Supplementary Deposits scheme or 'corset' was first introduced in 1973. It operated in this way: if banks expanded their IBELS (interest bearing eligible liabilities, i.e. deposits) too quickly they were called upon to make special deposits of cash with the Bank of England. Such deposits were non-interest bearing and could not be counted as reserve assets. The Bank set targets for the expansion of IBELS over a period. The greater the extent to which a bank overshot its IBEL target the greater would be the proportion of these extra liabilities the bank would have to place on deposit with the Bank of England. Hence the expression the 'corset' — the restrictions became tighter the faster the bank expanded its IBELS. At its most extreme the 'corset' could require a bank to deposit 100% of its extra IBELS with the Bank of England.

Although now suspended it is possible that the 'corset' could be reintroduced. It is also a technique which can be used for other purposes e.g. the West Germans have used it to discourage the deposits of foreign currency in German banks. (Score 1 mark for saying the 'corset' is a call for extra deposits of cash and 1 mark for explaining how the deposit was determined)

/2

10 We have already described the problem with short-term interest rates, and we will now consider the longer-term effects. Decreasing the interest rate may not encourage the investment but raising the interest

rate tends to *lock up liquidity* in the financial system. Businessmen, however, might still be willing to borrow at a relatively high rate of interest if they are sufficiently confident. This is because most *investment decisions are non-marginal*, that is the entrepreneur will be anticipating a sufficiently great return on his investment that small changes in the interest rate are unlikely to make a potentially profitable scheme unprofitable. The converse of this reasoning is that small falls in the interest rate are unlikely to turn unprofitable schemes into worthwhile ones.

In considering the effect of interest rates we must also take account of time on investment decisions; the *longer the term of an investment project the greater the proportion of total cost interest will represent.* We can illustrate this by an analogy with the individual consumer by asking which borrowing would be most influenced by the rise in the interest rate, borrowing to buy a car or a house? Obviously it is the house purchase, the long-term scheme.

Having mentioned house purchase we have touched on another problem and that is that governments may be unwilling to put up the interest rates because as so many voters are home-buyers, this is extremely unpopular.

There are other factors which make governments unwilling to face high interest rates. With a large national debt to service, raising interest rates increases their own expenditure. Similarly, with so many foreign deposits in the UK monetary sector, each percentage rise in interest rates means a drain of foreign currency on the balance of payments.

Despite these reservations, the 'normal' rate of interest has risen greatly over recent years. This may be partly attributed to inflation, but in a number of years in the 1970s interest rates did not keep pace with inflation so that the economy experienced negative 'real' rates of interest. In these circumstances it was understandable that people were still willing to borrow despite high nominal rates of interest. When in the 1980s interest rates remained high but the world economy was depressed, the effects were felt most keenly in less developed countries with their huge burdens of overseas debt to service. (Score 1 mark for each point in italics)

Your score

━━━━▷ *your total score for this Topic* . . . . /3
/20

Topic 6   Balance of payments

1   **Terms of trade** is a measure of the relative prices of imports and exports. It is calculated by taking the index of export prices and dividing it by the index of import prices (see Study Guide). The balance of trade, on the other hand, is the difference $(+)$ or $(-)$ between the value of imports and the value of exports. It is also known as the visible balance.

A favourable movement in the terms of trade i.e. a rise in the price of exports relative to imports, ought to improve **the balance of trade**. However before we can conclude this we would need to know such things as elasticity of demand for exports. (Score 1 mark each for describing the two expressions and 1 mark for explaining that a favourable movement in the terms of trade might not always be to the country's advantage)

/3

2   Each withdrawal and injection from the circular flow of income has a multiplier effect associated with it. In the case of foreign trade it is:

$$K = \frac{1}{MPM} = \frac{1}{m}$$

where K = the value of the multiplier and MPM or m = marginal propensity to import.

There is thus a multiplier effect upon the economy from any trade deficit or surplus. We are more familiar with the foreign trade multiplier when combined with others in the economy ie:

$$K = \frac{1}{s + t + m}$$

where s = marginal propensity to save and t = propensity to pay tax.

The value of this effect for the UK is a little less than 2. (Score 1 mark for explaining the effect of a deficit or surplus on the economy and 1 mark for the equation for the multiplier).

/2

3   A surplus of £9600m, i.e. using the coefficient of elasticity formula of $E = (\Delta Q/Q)/\Delta p/p)$ we obtain $1.2 = (x/80,000)/0.1 = 1.2 \times 0.1 \times 80,000 = x$; $x = £9600$.

Your score

/1

4   Devaluation or depreciation of the currency
Deflation of the economy e.g. budget surplus
Raising interest rates
Tariffs
Quotas
Non tariff barriers
Exchange control
Borrowing
Running down reserves of foreign currency
Improve productivity
(Score 1 mark for each two correct answers, up to a maximum of 3 marks)

/3

5   Having considered the list above you may realize that the cures fall into different categories. Devaluation or depreciation alter the *external* value of the currency but these are not an available measures if a nation is trying to maintain a fixed exchange rate. It must therefore consider the other measures. These we may divide between those that deflate the economy and those which try to protect the domestic economy. Deflationary measures try to work by altering the *internal* value of the currency. Protectionist measures may be used with either fixed or floating rates. However advocates of floating exchange rates (i.e. market forces) would tend to reject protectionist measures. (Score 2 marks if you explained the essential difference between internal and external measures)

/2

6   This problem can partly be considered by reference to the 1970s. In the mid 1970s the UK's balance of payments was in a parlous state. But then North Sea oil came on stream and in 1978 the price of oil increased massively. The UK's payments swung into surplus and the value of the pound soared. However, the increase in the price of oil was a major factor in plunging the world into depression. Thus, what seemed good for the balance of payments and for the pound was not necessarily good for the economy as a

whole. We are here faced with an interface of micro and macro effects. A price rise when demand is inelastic should increase income for oil producers (micro) but if oil prices are so significant in the balance of payments of oil-importing countries that it depresses their economies (macro) then the effects become uncertain.

The difficulty of predicting the effects of a price rise is complicated by the fact that all oil transactions are in dollars. This produces such anomalous effects as the fact that a fall in the value of the pound *increases* our earnings from oil.

/2

7   This can be viewed in two ways. First, the balance always balances in an accounting sense. Thus, for example, any imbalance will be made up by changes in official reserves of currency, or by borrowing. This results in an external balance of zero at the end of the year. However, viewed over a long period it becomes obvious that external accounts must always balance unless, as may be the case in less developed countries, other countries are simply willing to give them money. Thus, persistent deficits on current accounts must be balanced by surpluses on capital accounts and vice versa.

You should make sure that you fully understand the mechanism by which a balance is arrived at. (Score 1 mark for explaining the accountancy reasons and 1 mark for explaining that all external trade must eventually balance)

/2

8   This has been a significant item in the UK's balance of payments since the massive export of capital which took place in the nineteenth and early twentieth centuries. The income from these investments allowed the UK to balance considerable deficits on visible trade. However, the effect of two World Wars was to greatly reduce the UK's overseas investments. Thus, although interest profits and dividends are always a significant credit item and vitally important to the balance, the relative size of the surplus has substantially declined. This decline has been accelerated by the rise of inward investment in the UK since the Second World War.

Despite the relative decline in the UK's importance in international trade it is still a net exporter of capital and thus interest profits and dividends are likely to remain a net credit item. (Score 1 mark for explaining what the item is and that it is a net credit and 1 mark for charting its relative decline)

/2

9 Sterling balances is a term which is in common usage. It refers to *UK liabilities* (i.e. money owed) to non-residents which is denominated in sterling. There are two categories:
   (a) Official sterling balances — which are exchange reserves in sterling.
   (b) Private sterling balances — which are holdings of banking and money market liabilities in sterling.
   (To score your mark, you must make both points)

/1

10 The Keynsian (absorption) approach is based on the ability of the economy to respond to changes in the exchange rate. For example, it is argued that a depreciation will only be successful if there is spare capacity in the economy to *absorb* the extra demand created by the depreciation of the exchange rate. This approach centres on the current account (1 mark). The monetarist approach looks at the overall balance of payments and stresses the fact that there can only be a balance if the demand and supply of money, both internal and external are in equilibrium (1 mark).

/2

your total score for this Topic . . . . /20

Topic 7 Exchange rates

1 (a) Automatic stabilization of balance of payments.
   (b) Smaller need for reserves.
   (c) Frees internal policy from external constraints.
   (d) Absence of need for crisis meetings.
   (Score 1 mark for each two correct answers, no half marks)

/2

2 The bias of nationalism is when people believe that their country is always correct, its products always the best etc. The danger of this is that it can blind us to our own best interest, e.g. supporting an un-

realistically high exchange rate because we like to think of the pound as 'strong' whilst what we are in fact doing is benefitting foreigners by paying out high rates of interest etc.

3 If the demand for imports is perfectly unitary with respect to the exchange rate, i.e. each 1% depreciation in the exchange rate leads to a 1% drop in demand, or a 1% appreciation leads to a 1% rise in demand for imports, then the amount of pounds offered on the foreign exchange market will remain constant. Thus, whatever the exchange rate (price), the amount of pounds (quantity) remains the same. Plotted as the supply curve of pounds, this would give a vertical straight line (see p.154). (To score 2 marks you have got to get this absolutely right, otherwise you score zero)

/2

4 Score 1 mark if you said that differences in interest rates between countries will cause currency flows, thereby affecting exchange rates. Score a further 2 marks if you explained that expectations of changes in interest rates will also influence exchange rates and the premiums or discounts at which they are bought 'forward'.

/3

5 The argument on speculation is that it may either increase or decrease changes in exchange rates. Those who are of the opinion that it diminishes changes say that as rates rise speculators will speculate on the rate falling, i.e. by selling the currency, thereby diminishing the price rise. Conversely, if rates fall they speculate on a rise by purchasing the currency.

On the other hand in recent years it is hard to disagree that many of the changes in exchange rates have been *caused* by speculators.

/3

6 The 'crawling peg' was a variation on the adjustable peg system of the IMF. It allowed an exchange rate to 'crawl' upwards or downwards by a stated percentage each year.

/1

7 If there is a deficit then gold will be exported to bridge the gap. Since the money supply is determined by the quantity of gold in the country this will

cause the money supply to fall, this in turn reduces the price of British goods at home and abroad. Thus, foreigners will buy more British goods because they are cheaper and Britons will buy less imports because they are relatively dearer. Also, interest rates rise and thus encourage the inflow of money. The process continues until the deficit is eradicated and the pressure on the pound to depreciate ceases. (Score 1 mark for describing the export of gold and 1 mark for explaining the resultant deflationary process)

/2

8   A 'dirty float' is the expression used to describe the situation where whilst operating a freely fluctuating exchange rate, the government interferes covertly to manipulate the rate.

/1

9   Figure A·2 shows that the Americans now offer more dollars in exchange for pounds. Thus, the supply

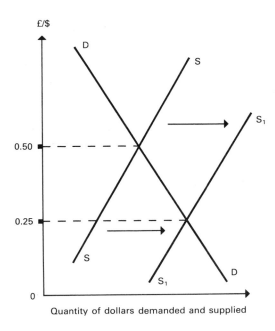

Fig. A.2

curve shifts to the right and the dollar depreciates. (In our example the exchange rate changes from £1 = $2 to £1 = $4!) You score 2 marks only if you got it absolutely right. It is essential that you understand this effect. There is, however, an alternative way of showing this effect. If you think that you got it right check on page 136. Check the labelling of the axes very carefully. Remember, no marks if you wrongly labelled the axes or left them off.

Your score /2

10   If we regard the international financial world as one market place, then we can see that investors will spread their assets between different countries to give themselves the greatest utility (Score 1 mark for this). The *portfolio balance theory* suggests interest rates are very important in determining exchange rates. (Score 1 mark) A variation on Modigliani's theory (Nobel prize winner 1984) would suggest that if any differences in earnings exist between countries then investors will continue to switch funds until it has been eliminated. (Score your third mark for explaining this effect)

/3

your total score for this Topic .... /20

Topic 8   International liquidity

1   We may define international liquidity as the assets of gold and foreign currencies held by the monetary authorities for the purpose of settling payment and imbalances and also for stabilizing exchange rates. (Score 1 mark for stating who holds the assets and the second mark for explaining the purpose of doing so)

/2

2   Score 1 mark each for any two of the following disadvantages:
   * it is expensive to store, protect and transport
   * it does not earn interest
   * it is very limited in supply
   * the physical supply is effectively controlled by very few countries e.g. South Africa and USSR

/2

3   The immediate reason for America's departure from the gold standard was massive balance of payments

*Your
score*

deficits and excessive dollar holdings overseas. These in turn were caused by the following factors:
* gold was undervalued
* inflation
* Vietnam War
* unwise reflation in order to win the presidential election

(Score 1 mark for the balance of payments and then 1 mark for any of the other points, up to a maximum of 3 marks)

/3

4 The main outcomes were:
(a) The demonetization of gold — i.e. the IMF and its members were supposed to phase out gold from international liquidity. This was partly done but the USA was later to regret its sales of gold. Other countries, such as France, held on to gold.
(b) Tacit recognition of the era of floating exchange rates — although members all agreed to try to move back towards pegged rates.

(Score 1 mark for each point)

5 The IDA is a subsidiary of the World Bank and was set up in 1960. Its object is to make loans for longer periods on preferential terms to less developed countries. It is also known as the 'soft loan window'.
(Score 1 mark if you stated the essential point that the IDA is to do with third world loans)

/1

6 The Organisation for Economic Cooperation and Development was set up in 1961. Its headquarters are in Paris.
Its main functions are:
* to encourage growth, high employment and financial stability amongst members
* to aid the economic development of less developed non-member countries.

(To score your second mark you must have correctly identified both functions — no half marks)

7 Score 1 mark for explaining that rescheduling of debt occurs when a debtor nation is no longer able to repay or service its overseas borrowing.
The most dramatic form of rescheduling would be for the country to default and simply refuse to pay its

debts (score a second mark for this). The problem for the country involved would be that no-one would ever lend it money again. Luckily no country has done this in recent years — Russia did in 1918 but that was rather a special case.

More likely, rescheduling would consist of a country renegotiating the terms of its loans and the rate of interest. Creditors may well agree to lowering the rate of interest if the only alternative is that the debtor nation defaults. (Score a third mark for explaining this) Rescheduling can apply to both government and private sector debts.

/3

8   In 1983 they were arranged like this:

	%
Dollar assets in USA	45.0
Euro dollars	18.0
ECUs	16.0
Currencies other than US dollar	15.0
Other eurocurrencies	6.0
	100.0

(To score your mark, you must have the order correct, we've given you the percentages for information. It's surprising how important ECUs are, isn't it!)

/1

9   The General Agreement on Tariffs and Trade was set up in 1948 and is the most important organization for the promotion of free trade in the Western World. It could be said that the two most important features of GATT were:
(a) that every signatory was to be treated as 'a most favoured nation', i.e. trading privileges could not be extended to one member without extending them to all. (Existing preference could continue.)
(b) Members agreed to work towards the reduction of tariffs and the abolition of quotas.

/2

10 Score 1 mark each for any two of the following reasons:
    * High interest rates
    * Excessive borrowing for balance of payments purposes rather than for specific projects

* Poor demand and low price of exports
* High price of oil (for non-oil exporters)

your total score for this Topic .... /20

Topic 9   Eurocurrencies

1   You will find that this point is emphasized in this topic. This is intentional because if you understand it then most of the rest is plain sailing. A eurocurrency is a *deposit in a bank* (or similar institution) which is *denominated in another currency*. For example, a deposit of pounds in a French bank, which continues to be counted as sterling, is a eurocurrency deposit. (If you have the two fundamental points of the definition score 2 marks; otherwise no marks at all!)

/2

2   In recent years major depositors have been:
* oil exporting countries e.g. Saudia Arabia
* multinational companies with a need for foreign currencies e.g. General Motors

/2

3   The three major European centres of the eurocurrency market are London, Luxembourg and Paris, whilst offshore there is Bahrain, Nassau, Singapore and Hong Kong. (Score 1 mark for each two correct, no half marks)

/2

4   A roll-over loan is a medium to long-term loan in eurocurrency, the interest on which is renegotiable at stated intervals e.g. 3 months. This interval is the roll-over. (Score one mark for explaining this and a second mark for the following.) Usually rates are linked to some agreed market rate e.g. LIBOR (London inter-bank offered rate) which is the most significant rate in eurocurrency dealings.

/2

5   Monetary policy can be adversely affected by the eurocurrency market in three main ways:
(a) The creation of excess liquidity in world currency markets leading to large flows of 'hot' money which may in turn: —
(b) Destabilise the exchange rate
(c) Flows of eurocurrency also affect the money supply causing it to expand or contract with little reference to domestic circumstances.

/3

6   Obviously, all domestic monetary authorities try to monitor what is happening in their own countries but the eurocurrency market demands a broader spectrum of measurement. Organizations which regularly attempt this are BIS and OECD. (Score 1 mark for each)

Your score

/2

7   Eurocurrency dealings are difficult to control because they are, by definition, international and there is no effective method of policing international banking. (Score 1 mark for explaining this)

    This is complicated by the fact that lenders often do not know who the ultimate borrowers may be and this is made more difficult by the huge growth in the debts of less developed countries. (Score a second mark for this point)

/2

8   A company may hold a eurocurrency deposit because it needs supplies of that currency in the future. But it may actually prefer a eurocurrency deposit if:
(a) the rate of interest is higher than domestic rates
(b) it can make a speculative gain because of changes in exchange rates.

/2

9   In 1985 the proportions of eurocurrency lending undertaken in the UK were

Other overseas banks in UK	45%
Japanese banks in UK	26%
US banks in UK	22%
London clearing banks	6%
Others	1%

Worldwide, (if one can say that of a eurocurrency market) it is the US banks which are the most important. (Your order must be exactly right to score your mark)

/1

10   Score 1 mark each for any two of the following answers:
* Restrictions on interest rates in the USA (e.g. Regulation Q) encouraging the export of dollars.
* USA balance of payments deficits in the 1960s.
* Dollar surpluses of OPEC countries in the early 1970s.

/2

your total score for this Topic . . . . /20

When you have completed all the short answer tests, fill in your scores on the score grid (inside the back cover). You can now use your results in this section to rank your revision priorities, starting with your weakest topic first.

Topics

For each topic, start with the study guide
and then try to answer the multiple choice
questions which follow.

Topic 1   The concept of money

Study guide

Almost every examination paper will have a question on the nature and functions of money. These we may summarize as:

Functions of money
1. Medium of exchange
2. Unit of account
3. Store of value
4. Standard of deferred payment

Attributes of money
1. Acceptability
2. Durability
3. Homogeneity
4. Divisibility
5. Portability
6. Stability of value
7. Difficult to counterfeit

Unfortunately it is very difficult to construct an answer on this topic which will appear fresh and original. However, since it is such a likely topic it is worth taking considerable trouble to prepare yourself. The problem is that most students simply list the functions and attributes above whereas something more is called for. You should try to start from an original or unusual angle to give freshness to your answer. Perhaps there is something in the morning paper to give you a start. If you are stuck for ideas here are two good starts.

What is money? That is a question which few people can answer, although nearly everybody thinks he knows the answer. It is reminiscent of the man who was asked to define an elephant, and could only reply that he would know one when he saw one.

Geoffrey Crowther *An Outline of Money*

Almost anything reasonably durable and portable can be used as money. But much modern money takes no physical form at all: it is merely represented by a row of figures in a bank ledger,or disgorged by a bank computer.

The Economist *Money and Finance*

Having constructed a good introduction you can then proceed to explain the nature and functions. Remember to illustrate each one with a suitable example.

A word of caution: Around 90% of people answering the questions on this topic will make reference to the crisis of the German Mark. Remember there were *two* crises —

(a) The hyperinflation of 1923 (money moved on wheelbarrows etc.)

(b) The collapse of confidence in the Mark 1945–47 (coffee and cigarettes used instead).

There is nothing wrong with these examples if properly used but why not try others? What about the present hyperinflation in Israel, for example, or the introduction of the pound coin?

An instructive definition is that of JL Hanson 'Money is what money does' (*Monetary Theory and Practice*). If you keep this *functional* definition in mind you cannot go wrong. However unlikely an asset may appear – camels, pigs' teeth, coffee — *if it fulfils the function of money then it is money*. Conversely a discredited bank note may look like money, smell like money and fold like money, but money it is not.

The fact that camels etc. may not be very good as money is to do with their attributes, not their functions.

Bank deposits as money

The majority of modern money is bank deposits. You should explain why bank deposits (which have no physical existence) are good as money whereas gold sovereigns are not. It may also be necessary to explain how money is 'created' by banks including the *bank multiplier*.

$$D = \frac{1}{r} \times C$$

Where **D** is the amount of bank deposits, **r** is the reserve ratio and **C** is the cash (or reserve assets) held by banks.

The effect of any additional deposit is given by the formula

$$\Delta D = \frac{1}{r} \times \Delta C$$

The bank multiplier can work either upwards or downwards.

Near money and quasi-money

Some assets have some of the attributes of money and fulfil some of its functions, but not well enough to be considered money. These may be termed *quasi-money*. For example, a postal order may be used as a medium of exchange, but its usefulness as such is limited. Other examples would be book tokens, luncheon vouchers and even building society deposits (see PSL 2 below).

Near money is any asset which can quickly be turned into money (without loss). Examples are Treasury bills, certificates of deposit and local authority bills. Near money assets provide *liquidity* for banks. They also comprise the main instruments which are dealt with in the money markets.

Inflation and the value of money

One of the most important attributes of money is stability of value. Inflation adversely affects this and therefore impairs the ability of money to fulfil its functions.

(a) **Store of value** is most badly affected. People may switch to other assets such as property, paintings or gold. Note however that savings ratio *increased* in periods of high inflation. Depending upon what we consider to be money, interest rates may (in part) compensate for the loss of value.

(b) **Standard of deferred payment.** Creditors may be reluctant to enter into long-term contracts. This may necessitate special clauses in contracts etc.

(c) **Unit of account.** This may make it difficult to compare values over time. The RPI is the usual measure of change in the value of money. Others include the CED and the GDP deflator. The existence of *constant price* schedules in the *National Accounts* are testimony to the problems caused.

(d) **Medium of exchange.** The most important function of money is the one least affected. Inflation will have to be extremely severe (hyperinflation) before money is not used. The most instructive feature of the German example of 1923 is that money was still used. Barter is terribly inconvenient.

Index-linking of financial assets

The rates of inflation in the late 1970s gave rise to the introduction of index-linked financial-assets. With these the capital value (principal) of the asset is linked to the rate of inflation (RPI). For example a Retirement Issue National Savings Certificate (Granny Bond) maturing over 5 years given an average rate of inflation of 10% p.a. and a 4% bonus on maturity would yield for an investment of £100:

Index-linking of principal

£100 × $(1.10)^5$	= £161.05
Plus bonus (4%)	6.44
	167.49

Such assets were attractive at times of high inflation but less so when inflation dropped and normal interest rates may exceed the yield on index-linked assets.

Index-linked assets have included Granny bonds, SAYE and some issues of gilts. At present most of these are being phased out.

Definitions of the money stock

There are a number of definitions of the money supply and of liquidity in the UK. You *must* be thoroughly familiar with these including some idea of their relative sizes. These may be found in the Bank of England Quarterly Bulletin and in most good textbooks. The definitions were modified in March 1984. The main effects of these changes was to exclude public sector deposits from M3 and to make the PSL 1 and 2 definitions more coherent with the M-type ones. The M0 definition was become more important as a policy objective.

You should be familiar with the following:

	M0	
Nib	M1	PSL 1
	M2	PSL 2
	£M3	
	M3	

(see Fig. A.1 on page 10)

The proliferation of definitions is caused by
— The need to conform with different concepts (operational balances, transactions, balances etc.).
— Search for a 'true' measure of money stock.
— Need to find a measure which 'behaved' as it should with respect to government monetary policy.

Such attempts at finding a 'true' measure are likely to suffer from Goodhart's law:

Any statistical regularity will tend to collapse once pressure is placed upon it for control purposes.

Further reading

Carter and Partington. *Applied Economics in Banking and Finance.* Oxford University Press. Chapters 2 and 6.
Crockett. *Money: Theory, Policy and Institutions.* 2nd edn. Van Nostrand Reinhold (UK). Chapter 1.

Hardwick, Khan and Longmead. *An Introduction to Modern Economics.* Longman. Chapter 21.

Lipsey. *An Introduction to Positive Economics.* Weidenfeld & Nicolson. Chapters 41 and 42.

Crowther. *An Outline of Money.* Nelson. Chapter 1 (a very old but classic text).

Beardshaw. *Economics: A Student's Guide.* Macdonald & Evans. Chapter 33.

Bank of England Quarterly Bulletin. (See March issue each year for all full definitions of money stock etc.).

The Economist. Money and Finance (Set of 10 briefs published jointly by the Economist and IoB).

Once you feel confident about your knowledge of this topic, try to answer the 10 multiple choice questions which follow.

Multiple choice questions

1 Which of the following is *not* a function of money? Money is:

  a readily acceptable.
  b a unit of account.
  c a standard of deferred payment.
  d a medium of exchange.

 *answer*

2 People accept a £5 note as money because they:

  a know that it is backed by gold.
  b know that it is legal tender.
  c realize that it would embarrass the seller if they refused to accept it.
  d believe others will accept it when they buy something from them.

 *answer*

3 Diamonds may not be considered as money because they are:

  a not durable.
  b unstable in conditions of supply.
  c non-homogeneous.
  d not easily portable.

 *answer*

4 With a reserve (or liquid asset) requirement of 20%, additional deposits of £1 million in a commercial bank will allow it to make additional loans of:

  a £800,000.
  b £1,000,000.
  c £4,000,000.
  d £5,000,000.

 *answer*

5 Money is 'created' by banks when:

   a they accept deposits of cash.
   b they make loans.
   c a bank loan given by one bank is redeposited in another.
   d they issue new cheque books.

 answer

6 Other things remaining constant, if the supply of notes and coins in the hands of the public goes up:

   a the total money stock increases.
   b the reserves of commercial banks decrease.
   c the reserves of commercial banks increase.
   d loans become easier to obtain from banks.

 answer

7 Which of the following may be considered as 'near money':

   a building society deposits.
   b luncheon vouchers.
   c gilt-edged securities.
   d commercial bills of exchange.

 answer

8 Which of the following would *not* result in an increase in the size of M2? An increase in:

   a notes and coins in circulation.
   b private sector non-interest bearing sterling sight deposits.
   c private sector sterling time deposits.
   d National Savings Bank ordinary accounts.

 answer

Questions 9 and 10 are based on the following items:

(i)   banks' till money
(ii)   private sector sterling time deposits (with original maturity of less than 2 years
(iii) private sector foreign currency deposits

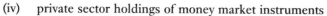

(iv)   private sector holdings of money market instruments
(v)   bankers' operational deposits at the Bank of England

9 Which of the above items are included in the M 3 definition of the money stock:

   a   (i), (ii) and (iii) only?
   b   (ii) and (iv) nly?
   c   (ii) and (iii) only?
   d   all of the items?

 *answer*

10 Which of the above items are included in the PSL 1 measure of liquidity:

   a   (i), (ii) and (v) only?
   b   (ii), (iii) and (v) only?
   c   (ii) and (iv) only?
   d   none of the above combinations is correct.

 *answer*

 Answers follow on pages 42–44. Score 2 marks for each correct answer.

Answers

1 The correct answer is **a**.

If this answer is not clear it is because you are confusing the *functions* of money with the *attributes*. It is a *function* of money to act as a medium of exchange; it is a necessary *attribute* of anything which acts as money to be readily acceptable. The medium of exchange function depends essentially on the concept of money and it is not even necessary for it to have a physical existence. For example one may effect a transaction with a *promise* to pay but money will still have fulfilled its function.

2 The correct answer is **d**.

People accept bank notes because they are *convenient* in the sense that they can be readily used to pay for purchases. It is a very long time (1931) since Bank of England notes were backed by gold (answer **a**). Answer **b** may seem tempting but it is only when bank notes are generally *unacceptable* (e.g. Germany 1945) that people consider their legal status. Answer **c** is obviously incorrect although the embarrassment of the *buyer* may be important in the seller accepting cheques.

3 The correct answer is **c**.

We are here concerned with the attributes of money. Diamonds are obviously extremely durable (answer **a**) and it is the fact that they are extremely *stable* in supply (i.e. very scarce) which gives them their value (answer **b**). It is also clear that they are easily transportable although security may be a problem. The problem is that diamonds differ greatly in quality and consequently in value and it is thus on homogeneity that they fail to be money. This is an instance of Gresham's law.

4 The correct answer is **a**.

If you got the answer wrong re-read the question — it is worded very carefully. The question asks how much in extra loans *it* will be able to make. You may have considered answer **c** to be correct. If so you have given the amount that the banking system as a whole may be able to create after loans and redeposits. If you chose answer **b** then you have forgotten that the bank must retain 1/5 of all deposits as liquid assets. With answer **d** you have not only forgotten to retain 1/5 of deposits but given the answer for the whole banking system as well.

5 The correct answer is **c**.

With answers **a** and **b** no credit creation is involved because the bank has just transferred money from lenders to borrowers. However when a loan is made and this is redeposited in a bank then the money supply has increased. If you chose answer **d** you should return to the fundamental definition of money and start again.

6 The correct answer is **b**.

Read the first part of the question carefully and you will realize that if the quantity of notes and coins in the hands of the public increases they must have withdrawn them from their bank accounts. Thus the money stock is unchanged (**a**). Banks have lost some of these reserve assets i.e. cash (answer **b**) so that answer **c** must be incorrect. Answer **d** is just tempting you to think that if the public has more cash in its hands then loans must be easier to get! Clearly nonsense.

7 The correct answer is **d**.

Building society deposits are either quasi-money or money depending on the money stock chosen (PSL 2 or M 3) (answer **a**). Luncheon vouchers are normally considered to be quasi-money (answer **b**). Gilt-edged securities are not considered to be either near-money or quasi-money (answer **c**). Commercial bills of exchange are near-money because they can very rapidly be liquified.

N.B. Not all texts make a distinction between near-money and quasi-money.

8 The correct answer is **c**.

Notes and coins in circulation are included in every definition of money stock or liquidity. Private sector non-interest bearing sterling sight deposits are in both the M 1 and M 2 definitions. M 2 is designed to measure the money available for 'transactions' purposes and therefore NSB accounts are included (answer **d**). Thus it is answer **c** which is correct since this is only included in the M 3 and PSL definition and therefore an increase in its size could not influence M 2.

9 The correct answer is **c**.

Answer **a** may seem tempting but in fact till money is excluded from the definition of M 3 though it is in M 0. In answer **b** (ii) is correct but item (iv) is only in the PSL 1 definition. In the correct answer (**c**) you may have been fooled by item (iii) which is excluded from £M 3 but not M 3. Clearly answer **d** is not possible.

10 The correct answer is **c**.

Although PSL 1 is a wide measure of liquidity till money and bankers' operational deposits are not included in it (**a**). In answer **b** item (iii) and (v) are incorrect. If you check the definition you will find that money market instruments held by the private sector are included in PSL 1 thus answer **c** is correct. Clearly therefore, answer **d** is not possible.

Score 2 marks for each correct answer. What was your score? Fill it in on the score grid.

If you scored 12 or less and are still a bit shaky on some points go back and look at the study guide again before proceeding any further.

If you are sure you really understand and are familiar with this topic now, try the 10 further questions which are on pages 190–192. Alternatively you can go on to your next topic and do all the post-tests together at the end.

Topic 2   The UK financial system

Study guide

This is a very large topic and one which you must know thoroughly. It encompasses the whole of the structure, function and operations of all of the financial institutions of the UK, ranging from banks to finance houses to the Bank of England. On the way through these notes you will be set several tasks. It is essential that you are able to do these. You will also find two diagrams and you must be able to describe all the **institutions** and **arrangements** shown in these.

The multiple choice tests will then be a way of checking that you know what you have learnt. You will also discover the importance of keeping up-to-date by reading newspapers and journals.

Financial intermediation

All the institutions described in these notes are **financial intermediaries**. This is the process by which funds are channelled from savers (the ultimate lenders) to ultimate borrowers via the working of third parties (financial intermediaries). The intermediaries include all banks, LDTs, insurance companies, finance houses and building societies. It is important to realize that financial intermediaries are more than go-betweens. They do not just act like employment agencies placing one lot of people in touch with another, other more important functions are involved. This was summarized by the Wilson Committee as follows:

When a financial institution intermediates it not only passes funds from lenders to borrowers, it usually also changes their terms and conditions. By aggregating small amounts of funds obtained from each of a large number of savers it is able to on-lend in larger packets, and often to transform *risk* and *maturity* characteristics.

There may be many steps along the way. Some financial intermediaries exist by borrowing from one lot of intermediaries and lending to another, e.g. discount houses.

We have mentioned two other functions **maturity transformation** and **risk transformation**. To illustrate these let us take an example. People deposit money in their current accounts which the bank promises to repay on demand — it then lends the money to a customer for a period of 3 years. Maturity transformation has taken place. But, if you were to lend your money directly to a friend to buy a car you would be taking a great risk. However, by taking many such risks and by the knowledge of its business the bank greatly reduces the risks. This is risk transformation.

In order to achieve these processes the bank must achieve the correct balance in its assets. There must always be enough cash to meet the day-to-day requirements of customers. It will then have a selection of liquid assets which it can quickly turn into cash if necessary. In order to make profits and/or to pay its depositors interest it must also have assets on which it earns a good income, sufficiently greater than the cost of the deposits it has attracted. Achieving the correct mix of assets is a complicated business. It depends upon the type of deposits the bank has accepted. The selection of assets must be appropriate to its liabilities and also acceptable to the monetary authorities. The principles which underly this ordering of assets are known as the **theory of portfolio balance**.

We have described the processes of financial intermediation. What do you suppose **disintermediation** means?

The monetary sector

We now turn to the definition of the *monetary sector*. This is all the institutions subject to the supervision of the Bank of England. This is defined by Monetary control-provisions 1981. The main sections are illustrated in Figure 2.1.

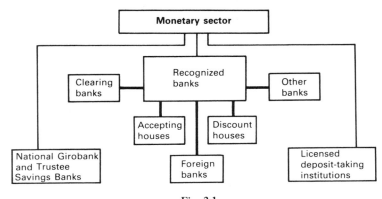

Fig. 2.1

Can you name at least one institution which is in the monetary sector which is not shown in the diagram?

There is likely to be some revision to these classifications as a result of the Johnson Matthey affair. It is possible that the classification LDT will disappear.

Commercial banks

Now compile a list of the main assets and liabilities of the clearing banks. Place the items in the order in which they would normally appear.

Exam tip: You *must* be able to do this and you should be able to describe the nature and function of each item. You should also be able to do the same for the following: building societies; finance houses; Accepting houses and discount houses. A tall order perhaps but a whole question may be devoted to any one of these.

All these institutions (except building societies) are subject to supervision by the Bank of England. The Bank licences all banks and LDTs and oversees their operations. The structure of a bank's assets must be acceptable to the Bank. Since 1981 the Bank has ceased to require the same reserve ratios of all institutions, it now demands that each institution's liquidity be appropriate to its business.

What ratios are still demanded of clearing banks? Did you remember the 5% of liabilities which must be with money market? If you said 6% you have missed the fact that this has been revised since 1981.

The Johnson Matthey Bankers affair of 1984 illustrated that supervision was still far from adequate. JMB collapsed after making loans which were too risky. It was rescued by the Bank of England.

Read up on the proposals for reform in the wake of the JMB affair. Proposals were first laid before Parliament 20th June 1984.

Capital adequacy

The suitability of a bank's assets structure may be referred to as its capital adequacy. The first principle is that banks should always have enough liquidity to meet the demands of their depositors. Secondly its capital (share capital, long-term loan capital and reserves) must be adequate to support the risk of losses on its assets. Risks could arise from bad debts (borrowers going into liquidation) and loss on investments when assets fall below their book value. Of course some risks are much greater than others. There is very little risk, for example, in holding UK Treasury bills whereas lending overseas may be regarded as more uncertain. One way to assess a bank's soundness, therefore, is to **weight** its assets according to the degree of risk. Those with high risk being highly weighted. This when compared with capital base would produce a **risk asset ratio**. The capital base demanded of a bank with lots of risky assets would be much greater than that of say a bank investing mainly in government stock. It now becomes clear why the Bank of England no longer lays down simple single ratios for all institutions. The Bank now makes **qualitative judgements** on the nature of a bank's business.

Foreign currencies

A particular feature of the UK banking system is the amount of foreign currency deposits. These are to be found both in UK banks and the branches of overseas banks in the UK (see answer to question 9 in Short answer test (p.11)). The risks are greater when dealing with foreign currencies because of the possibility of changes in the exchange rate. If a bank's total assets in one currency exceeds its total liabilities then it is vulnerable to a fall in the value of the currency. Whereas if its liabilities exceed it assets then it is likely to sustain a loss as a result of a rise in the value of that currency. The Bank has laid down guidelines on dealing. Roughly summarized they are that a bank should not have exposure in any one currency greater than 10% of its capital base and that short dealings (a bank's liabilities exceed its assets in a currency) in all currencies should not exceed 15% of the capital base. Different rules apply to overseas banks.

Profitability

You should be able to explain how changes in interest rates affect the profitability of banks. This will involve working through the balance sheet and considering the various items. Profitability will obviously be influenced by the distribution of the bank's assets. A great amount of fixed-interest loans will obviously reduce the profitability of banks if the interest rate rises. However, in recent years, rising interest rates have generally meant increased profits for banks. The ease with which banks can adjust their short-term assets in the money markets allows them to offset some of the adverse effects of any change in interest rates.

The money markets

The money markets are the places where money is 'wholesaled'. Traditionally the money market was concerned with the dealings between the discount houses, the clearers and the Bank of England. This is now known as the classical market. Since the 1950s many new markets have grown up such as the local authorities market. These are known as parallel markets. Figure 2.2 illustrates the main activities. The

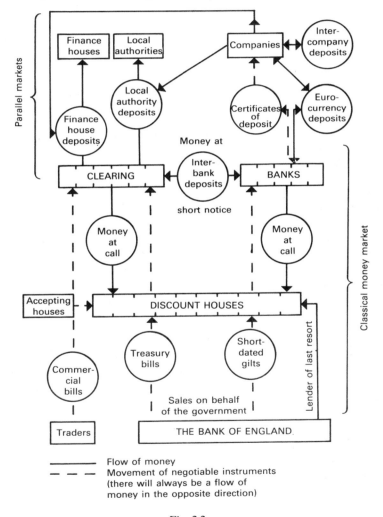

Fig. 2.2

items in circles represent financial instruments and those in boxes institutions. The discount houses also deal in all the parallel markets. Make sure that you fully understand all the terms and relationships in the diagram.

The Bank of England

Here are the main functions of the Bank of England:

— Government's banker
— Commercial bank
— Bankers' banker
— Operator of monetary policy
— Issuer of notes
— Adviser to the government
— Manager of national debt
— Supervisor of banks
— Lender of last resort
— Government's representative at IMF etc.
— Operator of the Exchange Equalisation Account

As a result of your previous studies you should be familiar with all of these. Could you write at least two paragraphs to describe each function?

 Write out the main items in the Bank of England Return (balance sheet) remembering to divide it into Issue Department and Banking Department.

Nearly all the functions of the Bank can be identified with items in the return. Try to do this. One of the important functions is that of banker's bank because it is in this way that inter-bank indebtness is adjusted via the clearing system. You should be fully familiar with this. There are many new developments such as BACS and CHAPS but these do not affect the way banks pay their debts to each other.

Gilts

You will also be required to know something about the gilts market. This is the buying and selling of government bonds. These are fixed interest bearing. (There are however some index linked gilts.) These are sold originally by the Bank of England on behalf of the government. They appear in the banks' balance sheet as 'investments'. They are important to the banks giving a secure earning asset. Short-dated gilts (less than 1 year to maturity) may be counted as liquid assets. They are also an important part of monetary policy, the Bank of England using their sale and (re)-purchase as a method of influencing the money supply and interest rates. This is known as open market operations.

Like many other things in the financial world much has changed in recent years. Until 1985 the Bank dealt only with 3 'stock jobbers' and half a dozen stockbrokers. It then proposed to widen the circle to 29 primary dealers with scores of secondary broker/dealers. The fixed commission on dealing was also abolished. The object of this was to increase competition. The market in London is large with a daily turnover of over £1 billion, although this is small by American standards where the daily turnover is over £50 billion.

Conclusion

The whole of the banking business can be seen as an attempt to reconcile profits and prudence. The banks wish to lend out as much money as possible in order to make profits but they must always ensure that they have sufficient liquidity to meet any demands upon them.

As we have seen in this and the previous unit much is changing in the financial world; definitions of the money supply, the supervision of banks, the gilts market and the Stock Exchange. This emphasizes the vital need for the successful student to keep up to date.

Further reading

Carter and Partington. *Applied Economics in Banking and Finance.* Oxford University Press. Chapters 3–6.

Crockett. *Money: Theory Policy and Institutions* 2 edn. Van Nostrand Reinhold (UK). Chapters 8 and 9.

Central Office of Information. *British Banking and Other Institutions.*

Committee of Review the Functioning of Financial Institutions (Wilson Committee). *Report*, HMSO.

Committee of London Clearing Bankers. *The London Clearing Banks — Evidence to the (Wilson) Committee to Review the Functioning of Financial Institutions.* Longman.

Shaw. *The London Money Market.* Heinemann.

Gerrard and National. *The London Discount Market.* Gerrard and National (available free on request).

Prest and Cappock. *The UK Economy* 9th edn. Pub. Weidenfeld & Nicolson.

Once you feel confident about your knowledge of this topic try to answer the 10 multiple choice questions which follow.

Multiple choice questions

1   Which of the following is an example of financial disintermediation:

   a   savers transfer money from banks to building societies?
   b   there is an increase in the amount of money going into endowment assurance policies?
   c   the inter-company market?
   d   depositors transfer money from current accounts to deposit accounts?

Questions 2–4 are concerned with the following assets of a UK clearing bank:

   (i)   special deposits with the Bank of England
   (ii)   operational deposits with the Bank of England
   (iii)   British government securities with less than one year to maturity
   (iv)   advances to customers

2   Which of the above items are accepted by the Bank of England as reserve (liquid) assets:

   a   (i) and (ii) only?
   b   (ii) only?
   c   (ii) and (iii) only?
   d   (i), (ii) and (iii) only?

3   Which of the above items would *normally* be classed as earning assets:

   a   (i), (iii) and (iv) only?
   b   (ii), (iii) and (iv) only?
   c   (iii) and (iv) only?
   d   (iv) only?

4 What is the correct order of liquidity of the above items (going from most to least liquid):

   a   (i), (ii), (iii), (iv)?
   b   (iv), (iii), (ii)?
   c   (ii), (i), (iii), (iv)?
   d   (ii), (iii), (iv)?

 *answer*

5 Which of the following best describes maturity transformation? The way in which:

   a   a bill of exchange automatically liquidates after a specified period.
   b   the yield of a financial asset varies in relation to its maturity.
   c   the Bank of England converts short term gilts into longer term gilts.
   d   banks convert short-term liabilities into longer-term assets.

 *answer*

6 The free resources ratio is the ratio of:

   a   current assets to capital resources.
   b   eligible reserve assets to eligible liabilities.
   c   assets available for loan to the total of loans outstanding.
   d   capital base to the adjusted total of risk assets.

 *answer*

7 The term 'liability management' means. The way in which banks:

   a   borrow money in the wholesale markets to match their demand for loans.
   b   maintain a graded portfolio of assets.
   c   undertake the management of the accounts of large customers.
   d   adjust their volume of loans to equate with the volume of deposits.

 *answer*

8 The National Savings Bank is popular with working people because it:

   a   has thousands of retail bank outlets (i.e. Post Offices).
   b   opens on Saturdays.
   c   gives tax free interest.
   d   gives a full range of services.

9 Which of the following best helps to explain the continued independent existence of the discount houses when, as long ago as the Radcliffe Report (1959) they were described as unnecessary? Is it that they:

   a   are highly profitable institutions?
   b   have expanded into many new areas of business?
   c   operate a monopoly of Treasury bill business?
   d   are protected by the Bank of England?

10 The Bank of England often sells gilt-edged securities through a firm of London stockbrokers. Which of the following functions of the Bank could this be an example of? Its function as:

   a   lender of last resort.
   b   operator of monetary policy.
   c   issuer of notes.
   d   manager of the Exchange Equalisation Account.

Answers follow on pages 55–59. Score 2 marks for each correct answer.

Answers

1 The correct answer is **c**.

It is perhaps a bit cheeky to ask about disintermediation instead of the more usual financial intermediation. However, the answer is quite straightforward. If financial intermediation concerns how banks etc. act as go-betweens for lenders and borrowers then disintermediation must be the process by which the ultimate lenders and borrowers avoid the intermediaries. In answer **a** depositors have simply moved their savings from one type of intermediary to another. This may affect the money supply figures but it does not involve disintermediation. Similarly in **b** the public is simply increasing its dealings with another set of financial intermediaries, the insurance companies. In the inter-company market (answer **c**) companies frequently lend directly to each other thus by-passing banks and others, avoiding the services of a financial intermediary. Answer **d** is, perhaps, the least likely answer of all since money has simply moved from one part of the banks' balance sheet to another.

2 The correct answer is **c**.

You really have to be totally familiar with a bank's balance sheet and everything to do with it. Thus, if you do not understand the answers to questions 2–4 you must go back to basics — *Elements of Banking* etc. — and study until you have made complete sense of it. Indeed as we have suggested, you should be able to write out the main items of a balance sheet from memory at the drop of a hat.

In question 2 the answer may appear difficult because there is now no published list of what is acceptable. However, as a rule of thumb, we may take the old reserve assets as a guide. Answer **a** obviously falls down because it includes Special Deposits which are, by definition, not liquid assets. Answer **b** is possible, so if you selected this one you are on the right track. However, answer **c** is better because short-dated gilts are normally considered liquid (or reserve) assets. If you chose answer **d** go back and start again. Advances have never at any time been considered liquid assets!

3 The correct answer is **d**.

The term earning assets is a little imprecise. However, a bank's balance sheet can normally be divided into those assets which are there primarily to give liquidity and those which earn money for the bank. Thus although some assets may earn interest e.g. Treasury bills, we would not normally class them as earning assets. The interest they earn is merely offsetting the cost of holding them rather than earning.

Answer **a** is tempting because all three do earn interest but Special Deposits earn a low rate (linked to Treasury bill rate) and banks would never choose them as a way of earning money. Indeed they will lose a great deal if the Bank of England calls for Special Deposits. Answer **b** is clearly incorrect since it includes the bank's operational deposits at the Bank of England which are non-interest bearing. If you chose answer **c** then you are on the right track. Indeed it could be argued that it is the correct answer. However, short-dated gilts usually have a low yield and are generally considered to give liquidity rather than earnings. Thus **d** is the correct answer.

4 The correct answer is **d**.

Has it ever occurred to you that banks' balance sheets are upside down? They arrange their assets from most liquid to least liquid. The items in the question are almost in the correct order except Special Deposits which normally appear half way through the balance sheet. Thus answer **a** cannot be correct since it classes Special Deposits as the most liquid. Since the Bank of England will not say when it will release Special Deposits they cannot, therefore, be liquid. Answer **b** puts the assets in reverse order from least liquid to most. If you chose this answer then clearly you have misunderstood the meaning of liquidity. Remember it refers to the *ease with which an asset may be turned into cash without loss*. It may seem that answer **c** is correct but since Special Deposits are, effectively, unusable, they cannot be as liquid as short-dated gilts thus this answer falls down. In answer **d** we have avoided the problem of Special Deposit by leaving it out of the list. The other items then fall easily into place. Deposits at the Bank of England are a bank's second most liquid asset after cash in hand. Gilts may quickly be sold (liquified) with little or no loss whilst advances are relatively illiquid. So here we have the correct order.

5 The correct answer is **d**.

Maturity transformation is at the heart of banking business. In essence banks borrow short (i.e. accept deposits) and lend long (give loans to customers). The other answers to this question all refer to different processes. Answer **a** describes the self-liquidating nature of a bill of exchange. In answer **b** we have a description of the yield curve which demonstrates how the yield of an asset varies in relation to its time to maturity. As far as answer **c** is concerned the Bank of England is indeed changing the maturity of the government liabilities but this need not directly affect the asset or liabilities of commercial banks. The process described in **c** is a 'funding' operation. The correct answer (**d**) summarizes the essence of banking business — accepting deposits (liabilities) and promising to repay them on demand and lending them to borrowers for longer periods of time. This is maturity transformation.

6 The correct answer is **a**.

This is a difficult question, in addition to which another of the answers (**d**) is very close to the correct answer. Therefore, do not be too upset if you got it wrong. The question is concerned with the capital adequacy of a bank. By this we mean having a suitable and acceptable asset structure. One of the ways of assessing this is the free asset ratio. This is defined in answer **a**. The Bank of England suggested a variation on this would be a gearing ratio:

$$\frac{\text{Capital base}}{\text{Deposits and other non-capital liabilities}}$$

Answer **b** describes the old reserve assets ratio which existed from 1971–1981. In answer **c** we have a relationship which has no particular name and is probably unquantifiable. Answer **d** defines the risk-assets ratio. This attempts to assess the capital adequacy in relationship to the risk of the loans (assets) which has been undertaken. The higher the value of the ratio the greater is the capital adequacy.

7 The correct answer is **a**.

The traditional view was that banks had to attract deposits before they could make loans. In recent years banks have been able to make loans and, where necessary, go to the wholesale (money) markets to borrow money to finance these. More specifically the term 'liability management' may be used to describe the situation where a bank has been approached to provide a term loan and it in turn seeks out a similar loan on the wholesale market. If this is the case then little in the way of maturity transformation is taking place, although risk transformation may be.

In answer **b** banks certainly do maintain a graded portfolio of assets so that some are constantly available to provide liquidity without loss. However, this is to do with the banks assets *not* liabilities. Banks may indeed concern themselves with the management of customers' accounts (answer **c**) but this is not liability management. Finally, in answer **d** we have the process known as 'asset management' which is, if you like, the opposite process to liability management.

8 The correct answer is **c**.

It is necessary for you to know details of all the financial institutions in the country. Thus a question on the NSB is quite in order. As far as this question is concerned **a**, **b** and **c** are all reasonable answers but **c** is the correct one. In answer **a** we could argue that despite this abundance of branches the NSB ordinary account business has continued to decline in relative terms. The same could be said of answer **b**. If you re-read the question carefully you will see that it refers to *working* people. For most taxpayers the NSB's Investment Accounts have offered one of the best-earning safe investments for the small saver. It is the Investment Account which has prospered over recent years. The government has granted its customers this privilege to encourage savers to save with it. As far as the last answer **d** is concerned, the NSB plainly does not give a full range of services so it is simply incorrect.

9 The correct answer is **d**.

You may be forgiven for getting this one wrong because all the responses, except **c** are true. However **d** presents the best explanation of why they still exist. The Monetary control-provisions of 1981 specifically require the clearing banks to maintain a proportion of their assets with the LDMA (London Discount Market Association), thus assuring the discount houses of funds. Thus the position of the discount houses is maintained.

They are indeed profitable institutions (answer **a**), but this under normal circumstances would probably have led to their activities being taken over by the clearers. The same could be argued for response **b** although it must be said that the discount houses are extremely adept both in the classical and parallel markets. Answer **c** is not true. If you chose this you are probably thinking of the cartel which the discount houses operated up to 1972, whereby they put in a combined tender for Treasury bills.

10 The correct answer is **b**.

Another correct answer would have been the Bank of England's function as Manager of the National Debt; however this was not an option and the answer must therefore be **b**. In acting as lender of last resort the Bank *buys* securities from the discount houses in order to put money into the system. Therefore for our question the transaction is the wrong way round. Similarly in answer **c** if the Bank uses more notes it is most likely increasing its stocks of gilts and not reducing them. Answer **d** has nothing whatsoever to do with the sale of gilts, so if you chose this one . . .! The Exchange Equalisation Account buys and sells foreign currency to help stabilize the exchange rate. It is possible, however, that stocks of sterling may be kept in the form of Treasury bills.

Score 2 marks for each correct answer. What was your score. Fill it in on the score grid.

If you scored 12 or less and are still a bit shaky on some points go back and look at the study guide again, before proceeding any further.

If you are sure you really understand and are familiar with this topic now, try the 10 further questions which are on pages 193–195. Alternatively you can go on to your next topic and do all the post-tests together at the end.

Topic 3   Interest rates

Study guide

The importance of understanding interest rates in monetary economics can hardly be overstated. Unfortunately it is a contentious topic with much disagreement over the fundamentals such as:
* The sources of interest
* Why people lend and borrow
* The effects of changes in interest rates upon the economy

We will deal with the first of these two in this section and the third when we look at monetary theory. You should realize however, that there are no clear cut answers and you must learn to evaluate the arguments. Fortunately we are agreed about most of the mechanics of interest rates and it is these we will consider first.

Different rates

Although politicians speak of 'getting the interest rate down' there are, in fact, many rates.

Here are a number of rates extracted from 'The Economist' 25 September 1985.

		%
Money market	Overnight	8.19
	3 months	11.50
Bond yields	Government	10.64
	Corporate	11.32
Eurocurrency	Bonds	11.44
	3 months deposits	10.94
Treasury bill		11.1
Bank deposit rate		7.75
Base rate		11.5
Eurodollar LIBOR 3 months		8.3

Define and explain these various rates.
Explain why they differ.

Reasons for different rates of interest

Do not make the fundamental mistake of saying interest rates depend upon whether you are borrowing or lending! All loans involve both a borrower and a lender. The person putting money into their bank account is lending money to the bank.

We can summarize the factors which influence interest rates like this:

Time preference. People have a preference for immediate consumption. Therefore the longer they are asked to refrain from using their income the greater the recompense they will require. We could describe interest as 'the reward for foregoing current consumption'.

The possibility of illiquidity. When people lend money they do it in return for some financial asset such as a Treasury bill. The rate of interest is influenced by the ease with which such assets can be resold. This helps explain why the interest on highly liquid assets such as CD's is lower than on less liquid assets such as debentures.

The possibility of default. The greater the risk the greater will be the rate of interest demanded.

Inflation. In times of high rates of inflation people will normally demand a high rate of interest.

Interest rates an the price of securities

It is essential to your understanding of interest rates that you realize that the rate of interest (or yield) and the price of securities are inversely proportional (i.e. move in opposite directions).

THE XYZ PLC

In return for the loan of £1000 promise
to pay £100 on 1 Jan
every year

Consider the above security. At face value it pays a rate of interest of 10%. However if market rates of interest fall to 5% then anyone possessing such an asset would be unwilling to sell it for £1000. Other things being equal the owner could demand a price of up to £2000 since £100 earning on £2000 is 5%. The reverse would happen if interest rates rose.

Naturally the relationship is not entirely mathematical since the rate of return is also affected by the factors discussed above, such as risk etc.

It is normal to describe the return on assets, as explained above as *yield* rather than interest. This is normally calculated as:

$$\text{Yield} = \frac{\textbf{par value} \times \textbf{earnings}}{\textbf{market price of security}}$$

Example: Suppose the market price of the XYZ security above were to be £666. This would give a yield of:

$$15\% = \frac{£1000 \times 0.10}{£666}$$

Check your understanding of this idea by answering the following questions based on the XYZ security.

What would be the yield if the price of the security were:
- a £400
- b £1600
- c £1800

Discounting other factors what would be the market price of the security if the yields were:
- d 12.5%
- e 2.0%
- f 7.5%

You'll find the answers at the bottom of the page.

Now look at the first task in this section again. To what extent does the above explain the differences. NB: several of the rates are yields rather than interest rates.

Yield curve

A yield curve plots the yield of the same type of asset but with different maturity dates. Under normal circumstances the yield rises with maturity. Expectation of changes in interest rates can vary the shape of the curve.

a Construct a normal yield curve.
b How would it vary if investors believed that interest rates would rise in the future?

If you are not sure of an answer to a problem check with the answer to multiple choice question 3.1.

a 25% b 6.25% c 5.55% d £800 e £5000 f £1333 Did you get the right answers? If you didn't then recheck until you can obtain the correct answers.

Nominal and real rates of interest

At the end of a period of a loan the lender then receives the repayment of the capital as well as the rate of interest. If there has been inflation this will have decreased the value of the capital; so in order to obtain the *real rate of interest* we need to subtract the rate of inflation. It is possible for the real rate of interest to be either positive or negative. It was negative for most of the 1970s.

In simple terms; if nominal rates of interest were 10% and inflation 5% then the real rate of interest should be 5%. But if, for example someone deposited £100 at the beginning of the year after 12 months they would need this to have increased in value to £105 to keep pace with inflation. Thus in our example the £5 earned above this is actually interest on £105 not on £100 thus the real rate of interest is 4.76%. (You can check your understanding of this point in multiple choice question 3.3.)

The government and the rate of interest

According to all schools of thought, to a greater or lesser extent, raising the rate of interest should restrict the economy, discouraging investment and so on. Conversely lower interest rates should stimulate the economy. Thus governments will be very concerned about the rate of interest and they have long been considered an important part of monetary policy. Several points should be considered:

* Governments cannot change interest rates significantly at will. The market will reassert itself.
* Nonetheless the government significantly influences rates because it is the chief borrower in the economy and the controller of the currency.
* International pressures may thwart the best-laid plans of government

Governments can affect interest rates through the usual methods of monetary policy (see Study guide in Topic 5). However desire to control the interest rates may conflict with other objectives of policy such as the desire to control the money supply. In the period of the Conservative government after 1979 such was the desire to control the money stock in order to restrain inflation that the government was willing to put up with high interest rates even when these were admitted to be damaging the economy.

Since interest is the price of money the most fundamental principles of economics tell us that the government cannot control the supply *and* the price of money simultaneously.

Discussions of interest rates and the governments role centre around the PSBR. Several points must be borne in mind:

(a) High levels of borrowing will lead to high levels of interest rates as the government lowers the price of assets to make them more attractive.

(b) 'Crowding out' may occur as government borrowing starves other sectors of the economy of funds.

(c) A high level of interest on long-dated gilts is likely to increase long-term interest rates in the rest of the market; with corresponding deleterious effect upon the economy.

(d) The effect of increased government borrowing will vary according to whether the money is borrowed from the general public or the banking sector. Increased sales to the non-bank private sector are generally supposed to increase interest rates.

NB The success of the Conservative government in cutting the real size of the PSBR but the failure to reduce real interest rates underlines the importance of international factors and uncertainty in determining interest rates.

The theories of the interest rate

We will now examine the poles of the argument on interest rates. To understand these you must realize that there is fundamental disagreement about the demand for money, i.e. the desire of people to hold money in the form of cash or bank deposits.

Monetarist theory of demand for money

Monetarists believe that there is a dividing line in the portfolio between money and other assets. Thus we can say that money and other financial assets are *not* close substitutes for one another. However, monetarists would state this condition in the following form: *Money is a substitute for all assets alike, real and financial, rather than a close substitute for only a small range of financial assets.* From this, monetarists state that the demand for money is *stable* and *predictable*, being determined by spending and income. This is in sharp contrast to the Keynesian view. (See Fig. 4.3, p.80.)

Keynesian theory of the demand for money

Keynes argued that on some occasions people might wish to hold (demand) money as an asset. He said that there were three motives for demanding money; the transactions, precautionary and speculative motives.

(a) **Transactions motive.** People hold cash and money in bank accounts simply to carry on the everyday business of life — to pay the gas bill, to buy petrol, to spend on groceries and so on. Since people are usually paid weekly or monthly but spend money daily they therefore have to hold a proportion of their income as money.

What determines the size of transactions demand for money? The answer is income. The higher the level of income the higher will be the transactions demand for money. The reason for this is simply that with a higher income people spend more; they may, indeed, spend a smaller proportion of their income but they nonetheless spend more money and this creates a greater demand for money.

There is no disagreement between Keynesians and monetarists on this point, other than one of terminology. Monetarists would say that the demand for money is determined by the **transmission mechanism** rather than the transactions motive.

(b) **The precautionary motive.** People hold money in bank accounts etc. to guard against unexpected eventualities — the car breaking down, a period of illness, a large electricity bill, and so on. Again we can see that this demand will increase with income. The higher the level of income the higher will be the size of precautionary balances.

The reason for this is that the rich need higher precautionary balances; if, for example, you are running several cars and a large house, then the unexpected bills are likely to be much larger, thus demanding a larger precautionary stock of money.

The precautionary motive and the transactions motive thus act in the same manner with respect to income, so that we may lump them together.

(c) **The speculative motive.** It is with the speculative motive that we reach a key difference between the monetarists and the Keynesians. Monetarists do not think that people will want money for itself but only for transactions purposes. Keynes, however, believed that people might speculate by holding money, just as they might speculate with other assets. The speculative demand for money is that money which is held in hope of making a speculative gain as a result of the change in interest rates and the price of financial assets.

To understand this fully it is necessary to appreciate that the price of securities and the rate of interest are inversely proportional to each other as was described above.

Keynes also believed that investors had a concept of the **normal rate of interest.** If the rate of interest was below this then people would

speculate by holding cash, anticipating that interest rates would rise and bond prices fall. Thus low interest rates are associated with a high speculative demand for money. Conversely then, if the rate of interest was high, people would buy bonds because their price would be low and their earning high. Investors also stand to gain if the interest rate falls and bond prices increase, because they could then make a capital gain by selling them. Thus a high rate of interest is associated with a low demand for money. Other things being constant, the rate of interest and the speculative demand for money are inversely proportional to one another.

Liquidity preference

If we aggregate these three demands for money (transaction, precautionary and speculative) then it gives us the community's total demand for money at any particular time. This is known as their liquidity preference i.e. their demand to hold money as opposed to bonds or other assets.

Figure 3.1 illustrates a liquidity preference schedule. In the diagram curve L is the community's demand for money at any particular interest date. The transactions and precautionary demand are little affected by interest rates. In Figure 3.1 OA could be said to be the demand attributable to these motives. To this is added speculative demand, which is inversely proportional to the rate of interest and therefore gives us a downward-sloping liquidity preference schedule (L).

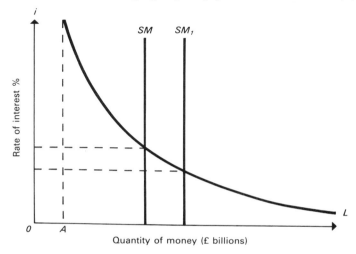

Fig. 3.1

At low levels of interest the liquidity preference schedule flattens out, showing that it has become perfectly interest-elastic.

In Figure 3.1 SM represents the stock of money. This being the case, the interaction of SM with L forms the rate of interest. An increase in the stock of money to SM_1 has the effect of decreasing the interest rate, *ceteris paribus*.

Conclusion

As a student you may legitimately ask which theory is correct. The answer is that neither is completely satisfactory. The monetarist theory places emphasis on the supply of money and neglects demand whilst the situation is reversed for the Keynesian theory. Whilst to this we must add our knowledge of the government and international influences, a fundamental difference remains.

— For the monetarist the rate of interest is an equilibrium price bringing the forces of demand and supply for funds in the economy into equilibrium thereby ensuring the full employment of all resources.

— Keynes's point of view admits the possibility of disequilibrium believing that people may hold onto money thus leaving resources unused and therefore causing unemployment.

We examine further consequences of these disagreements in the next topic.

Further reading

Crockett. *Money: Theory, Policy and Institutions* 2nd edn. Van Nostrand Reinhold (UK). Chapter 3.

Griffiths and Wall. *Applied Economics.* Longman. Chapter 16.

Carter and Partington. *Applied Economics in Banking and Finance.* Oxford University Press. Chapter 7.

Beardshaw. *Economics: A Student's Guide.* Macdonald & Evans. Chapters 23 and 36.

Once you feel confident about your knowledge of this topic try to answer the 10 multiple choice questions which follow.

Multiple choice questions

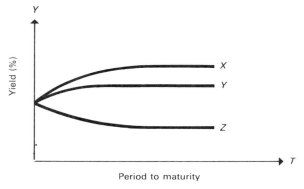

Fig. 3.2

1 The graph marked Z in Figure 3.2 shows a situation where there is an expectation that interest rates are likely to:

   a fall.
   b rise.
   c remain constant.
   d remain constant for a while and then rise.

2 If a company borrows money from a bank on overdraft and lends this money on the money market at a higher rate this is an example of:

   a bed and breakfasting.
   b round tripping.
   c differential term structure.
   d insider dealing.

3 Which of the following represents the most accurate way to calculate the real rate of interest. The real rate of interest equals:

   a the normal rate of interest minus the rate of inflation.

   b $\dfrac{\text{par value} \times \text{dividend}}{\text{market price of asset}}$.

c $\dfrac{\text{original deposit} + \text{rate of interest}}{\text{rate of inflation}}$.

d $\left[\dfrac{1 + \text{nominal rate of interest}}{1 + \text{rate of inflation}}\right] - 1.$

answer

4   The Reverse Yield Gap refers to the fact that:

    a   yields on equities are below the yields on gilt edged stocks.

    b   the real rate of interest may be negative in times of high inflation.

    c   the yield on securities is inversely proportionate to their price.

    d   in times of inflation debtors see the real burden of their debt reduced.

answer

5   Suppose that £100 was deposited in a building society and received 8% p.a. net of tax for 5 years. If none of the interest were withdrawn what would be the total value of the deposit after 5 years? Would it be:

    a   £140?

    b   £146.93p?

    c   £148.29p?

    d   £158.68p?

answer

6   Which of the following provides the best explanation for why people may be willing to accept negative real rates of interest on such investments as gilt edged securities:

    a   they expect interest rates to fall in the future?

    b   other investments are not available?

    c   government securities are very risk free?

    d   they expect that the price of gilt edged securities will fall in the future?

answer

7   The expression the 'liquidity trap' refers to:

   a   the way raising interest rate 'locks up' investments.
   b   financial intermediaries lending too large a portion of their assets for long periods.
   c   the demand for money becoming interest-elastic at very low rates of interest.
   d   money trapped by the speculative motion in anticipation of a rise in interest rates.

8   Keynes's liquidity preference theory of interest rates differed from the flow of funds explanation in that Keynes:

   a   did not accept the transactions demand for money.
   b   maintained that the demand for money and the rate of interest were inversely related to one another.
   c   suggested that people would never wish to hold money for its own sake.
   d   believed that disequilibrium was possible between saving and borrowing.

9   If the government significantly increases the size of the PSBR this is likely to lead to a:

   a   fall in interest rates if it is accompanied by a budget surplus.
   b   rise in interest rates if the borrowing is mainly from the non-bank private sector.
   c   fall in the money supply if the borrowing is mainly from banks.
   d   rise in the liquidity of the banking sector.

10 Which of the following is the likely action of a commercial bank following a decline in market interest rates:

   a   a cut in the level of bank charges to attract more depositors?
   b   a rise in deposit rates to prevent customers switching to building societies?

c the development of alternative services such as investment management?

d an increase in disintermediation?

 answer

Answers follow on pages 72–76. Score 2 marks for each correct answer.

Answers

1   The correct answer is **a**.

Here we are concerned with the yield curve of financial assets. This measures the yield (*not the rate of interest*) of similar assets against their time to maturity. If an asset is very near to maturity (whatever its original maturity) then its yield will be very close to short-term interest rates such as those in the money markets. Those assets which are not due to mature for 6 months or so will have a higher yield to compensate owners for taking the risk of having their money tied up. Those not due to mature for 2 years a slightly higher yield and so on. This state of affairs is shown by curve Y (answer **c**).

If investors anticipate that interest rates are likely to rise in the future then they will demand a higher yield if they are going to tie their money up in longer dated assets. This will therefore augment the yield curve. This is shown by curve X (answer **b**). Conversely if investors anticipate that interest rates will fall then they will be willing to hold longer dated assets with lower yields believing that such good rates will not be available in 6 months or so. This is shown by curve Z (the correct answer **a**). A situation such as Z is termed a perverse yield curve.

Answer **d** is simply a variation on situation **b**.

2   The correct answer is **b**.

This is a question on financial jargon which you either know or don't. If you are unfamiliar with these terms then this is evidence that you are not reading the financial press regularly. In this subject it is absolutely essential that you get into the habit of reading a major newspaper *every day*.

'Bed and breakfasting' is a stock market term and refers to selling shares one day and buying them back the next (answer **a**). The correct answer **b**, 'round tripping', can also be termed **money market arbitrage**. The term arbitrage can be applied to other situations where it is possible to make profits by buying and selling between two differing market rates, e.g. in foreign exchange markets.

'Differential term structure' (answer **c**) is a term we made up and has no meaning. The final answer (**d**) is again a stock market expression. It refers to a situation where a person with inside knowledge of takeovers etc. uses it to make a killing. It is forbidden by Stock Exchange rules.

3   The correct answer is **d**.

If you chose answer **a** then you have chosen the normal 'rule of thumb' definition of the real rate of interest. This is quite accurate enough except in times of very high rates of inflation and interest rates. It is normally adopted because of the mathematical complication of the truly accurate method. Answer **b** is the formula for calculating the *yield* on a financial asset. The suggested answer **c** is nonsense and does not correspond to anything at all. We hope you didn't choose this one!

Suppose that the nominal rate of interest is 14% and that inflation is running at 10% then the real rate of interest is money earned after making allowance for the earnings necessary to keep pace with inflation. In simple terms, if £100 were deposited at the beginning of the year then by the end of the year it would be worth £114. This would appear to be a real earning of £4 or 4% (answer **a**). *But* in order to just keep pace with inflation the deposit would have to grow to £110. Expressed as a percentage of this figure the real rate of interest is therefore lower. Following the formula given in answer **d** we obtain

$$\left[\frac{1 + 14}{1 + 10} \right] - 1$$
$$= 0.03636$$
$$\text{or } 3.6\%$$

4 The correct answer is **a**.

The Reverse Yield Gap is another technical expression of the financial markets and is defined in answer **a**. It is termed a reverse yield gap because traditionally the yield on equities was higher than that on fixed interest securities but in recent years such things as gilt edged stocks have tended to give a bigger return thus 'reversing' the position. All the other answers are true but do not refer to yield gaps. Answer **b** describes the condition of negative real rates of interest. In **c** we are describing the normal relationship between the yield of a security and its price. This is a relationship you must fully understand if you are to make sense of the rate of interest. Answer **d** describes how debtors see the real burden of their debt reduced if inflation increases their incomes.

5 The correct answer is **b**.

This is a straightforward question concerning compound interest. With possibility **a** we have the answer in terms of simple interest, i.e. interest of 8% on £100 is £8 multiplied by 5 and would give us the figure of £140. However after 1 year the deposit would be worth £108 and 8% added to this would give a value for the second year of £116.64 and 8% on top of this would give a value of £125.97 for the third year and so on. Thus we reach the value of £146.93 after 5 years.

Possibility **c** is simply an incorrect calculation whereas possibility **d** gives the answer after 6 years.

6 The correct answer is **a**.

The chief reason why individuals may be willing to accept negative real interest is to be found in the motives for thrift and precautionary balances. The reason for institutions accepting negative rates are more complex. One such reason is given in answer **b**. Thus if you chose **b** you are correct as far as institutions are concerned.

Possibility **c** is certainly true but not directly relevant to the question. Indeed the government had to introduce index-linking of assets to encourage people to hold them when rates of inflation were high.

In answer **d** we have the opposite of answer **a** because, you will recall the price of securities and the rate of interest vary inversely with one another. Thus in **d** if people expect the price of securities to fall they are expecting the rate of interest to rise and will thus hold on to their money. Conversely in the correct solution (**a**) an expectation of falling rates of interest will encourage people to hold financial assets because opportunities will be even worse in the future. In addition to this a fall in interest rates will increase the price of the financial assets they hold thus giving the possibility of a capital gain.

7 The correct answer is **c**.

Here we are concerned with a theoretical aspect of the syllabus but one which you should fully understand. To understand the correct answer you must be familiar with the liquidity preference curve (schedule) and/or the LM curve. If they become flat at low rates of interest this implies that increases in the money stock may not increase national income but simply leave money unlent or 'trapped'. This may also be termed the 'depression pole' of the economy. It should be pointed out that this is a Keynesian view and disputed by monetarists. Nonetheless you must be able to explain the liquidity trap.

In answer **b** banks and others will find themselves in a liquidity crisis but this is not called the liquidity trap. Answer **a** is also true but not relevant to the question. Raising rates of interest makes banks and others very reluctant to sell financial assets since they would make a capital loss. They will, therefore, hold on to assets in the hope of a fall in interest rates thus 'locking up' investments. Answer **d** describes the situation in which people will hold on to money if interest rates are low expecting that interest rates will rise and the price of securities fall. This again is a Keynesian view.

8   The correct answer is **d**.

Answer **a** is incorrect in that all schools of thought accept the transactions demand and all agree that it varies directly with income. Keynes did indeed maintain that the demand for money varied inversely with the rate of interest (**b**), but then so did the classical school. The difference was that Keynes maintained that the demand for money was more responsive to interest rate changes than his classical opponents, or monetarists today.

With answer **c** we have one of the key differences between Keynes and the flow of funds school in that Keynes *did* say that people would wish to hold money for its own sake if interest rates were low. This is the speculative demand for money.

The one key difference between Keynes and the classicists and today's monetarists is that Keynes maintained that disequilibrium was possible (see answer to previous question). The classical school believed that the economy was self regulating; Keynes disagreed with this. To the classical school the rate of interest was a price which would automatically bring saving and borrowing and ultimately the whole economy into equilibrium with each other. Crucial to Keynes view was his realization that people could 'invest' in either new projects or 'old' investments such as existing government bonds. If only new investment were possible there would be an equilibrium but since the possibility of 'old' investments existed this could leave existing resources idle and hence create disequilibrium.

9   The correct answer is **b**.

Answer **a** is nonsense since a rise in the PSBR must mean that there is a budget deficit. Thus, although a budget surplus might possibly lead to a fall in interest rates it is not possible under the conditions stated.

If the government finances the increase in the PSBR by borrowing from the banking sector (answer **c**) then this will lead to an increase in the money supply. This is because the banks may use the assets acquired to further extend their lending. The effects of increasing the size of the PSBR upon the liquidity of the banking sector are uncertain (**d**), depending upon how the PSBR is financed.

Answer **b** is the most probable since the government is likely to have to increase interest rates on government securities in order to encourage people to lend it more money. Also increased sales of securities will decrease their price and hence increase the rate of interest.

10   The correct answer is **c**.

Answer **a** is the opposite of the true answer because a fall in interest rates will decrease banks' profitability and cause them to look for other ways to increase their income, for example by raising charges. Answer **b** is also incorrect since banks will have to cut deposit rates. This is because their lending will now be earning less money and they will be forced to offer lower rates to depositors.

Of the options provided answer **c** presents the only way in which banks may increase their income to offset the fall in interest rates. Answer **d** is a non-starter since banks are, by definition, concerned with intermediation not disintermediation — any increase in the latter would decrease their profits.

Score 2 marks for each correct answer. What was your score? Fill it in on the score grid.

If you scored 12 or less and are still a bit shaky on some points go back and look at the study guide again before proceeding any further.

If you are sure you really understand and are familiar with this topic now, try the 10 further questions which are on pages 195–198. Alternatively you can go on to your next topic and do all the post-tests together at the end.

Topic 4   Monetary theory

Study guide

Look at the diagram below. Here we have a collection of areas of interest all of which are relevant to our understanding of the economy. Work your way round the outside of the diagram and make sure that you know what all the terms mean and how they relate to monetary theory.

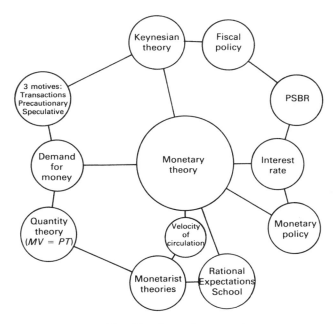

Fig. 4.1 *Aspects of monetary theory*

We cannot reconcile all the items because there are profound disagreements about the nature of monetary theory. The fact that the greatest economists in the world differ on these subjects teaches us that we understand the problems imperfectly. It is therefore necessary for us to understand all these ideas.

The equilibrium of national income

The conventional picture of the economy is still that presented by Keynes. This is illustrated in Figure 4.2. Here the equilibrium of national income occurs where the AMD or C + I + G + (X − M) line crosses the 45° line.

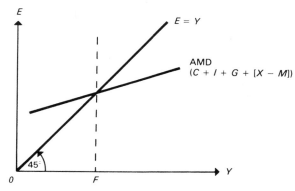

Fig. 4.2

In the diagram in Figure 2 if O F is the full employment level of national income demonstrate:

a   an inflationary gap
b   a deflationary gap.

In the diagram OF represents the full employment level of national income and the equilibrium has occurred at full employment. Keynes maintained that the equilibrium level was fortuitous and could result in either inflation or unemployment.

The fact that these are seen as opposites in Keynes's view goes a long way to explain the dissatisfaction with the theory in the recent years of combined unemployment and inflation.

Why monetarism?

The rise of monetarist ideas was brought about by the inability of Keynesian economics to explain or to cure the seemingly contradictory problems of rising unemployment and inflation. Not only did monetarists seek to explain contemporary problems; they reinterpreted historical ones. Milton Friedman and Anna Schwartz in their book, *A monetary history of the United States, 1867–1960* argued that the depression of 1930 was caused by a *contraction* of the money supply and not by lack of investment as Keynes had argued. They also maintained that post-war inflation was caused by *over-expansion* of the money supply. This gave rise to their famous statement 'inflation is always and everywhere a monetary phenomenon'.

Monetarists argue for control of the money supply to avoid both inflation and depression; neo-Keynesians, on the other hand, concentrate on fiscal policy. However, within both camps there are many shades of opinion. In practice there is a considerable degree of overlap between the two philosophies, so that an economist can lean towards monetarist ideas on some matters and towards Keynesianism on others.

Keynesians and Monetarists defined

Monetarists are those who believe that changes in the money supply cause changes in national income, while the neo-Keynesians maintain that changes in national income bring about changes in the money supply. We are here speaking of **nominal national income** i.e. national income at current prices. However, we can also speak of **real national income** i.e. discounting the effect of changes in the price level. If we restate the propositions in terms of real national income the implications become significantly altered.

Monetarists believe that changes in the money supply can have only small and temporary effects upon *real* national income; in the long-run, changes in the money supply will only result in changes in the price level. The neo-Keynesians believe that changes in the money supply can bring about changes in real national income. Monetarists do believe, however, that it is possible for overexpansion of the money supply to cause unemployment if prices are inflexible downwards.

Construct a diagram plotting the rate of inflation on the vertical axis against the rate of unemployment on the horizontal for the period of the last 15 years.
* Does the diagram support the idea of a trade-off of inflation against uemployment?
* How would monetarist and Keynesian explanations of the diagram vary?

Hint. We are speaking here of the expectations augmented Phillips Curve. (See Post-test 4, multiple choice question 6.)

The theory of portfolio balance

In the last section of the study guide we explained that there is a difference between the Keynesian and monetarist theories of the demand for money. This we may now expand into the theory of portfolio balance.

All schools of thought agree that people will try to obtain the greatest possible use from their assets. The differences are illustrated in Figure 4.3.

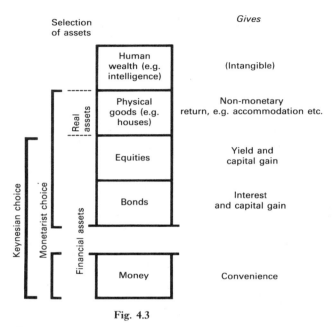

Fig. 4.3

Contrast the monetarist and Keynesian views of the effect of an increase in the interest rate upon portfolio balance.

IS and LM curves

To some extent the differences between the schools of thought may be reconciled on IS and LM curve analysis.

The IS curve shows all the combinations of the rate of interest and the level of income at which the real economy is in equilibrium. The LM curve, on the other hand, shows the relationship between all of the points at which the monetary sector of the economy is in equilibrium, i.e. the demand for money equals the supply of money and the rate of interest.

The equilibrium is illustrated in Figure 4.4. IS and LM curve equilibriums are a method by which we may investigate the effect of both real and monetary changes upon the economy.

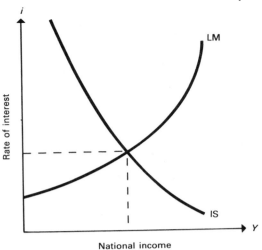

Fig. 4.4

We may summarize the possibilities thus:

Budget deficit → Rightward shift in IS → Y increases, i increases
Budget surplus → Leftward shift in IS → Y decreases, i decreases
Money supply expanded → Rightward shift in LM → Y increases, i decreases
Money supply contracted → Leftward shift in LM → Y decreases, i increases

We can summarise the difference in opinion by saying that monetarists argue that the IS curve tends to be flat while the LM curve is steep and the Keynesians argue the reverse. These possibilities are shown in Figure 4.5.

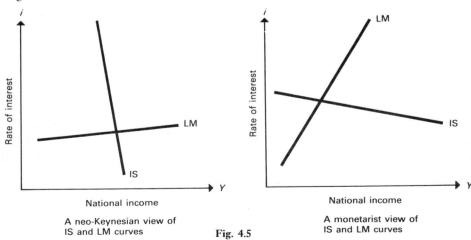

A neo-Keynesian view of
IS and LM curves

Fig. 4.5

A monetarist view of
IS and LM curves

81

The monetarist argument

Monetarists argue that the IS curve is relatively flat because the level of investment is responsive to changes in the rate of investment. Thus, a small fall in the rate of interest would cause a large rise in national income. Conversely, it is argued that neither demand nor supply of money is greatly affected by changes in the interest rates. This has the effect of making the LM curve very steep.

Neo-Keynesian arguments

The neo-Keynesians argue that the IS curve is steep because investment is *not* very sensitive to changes in the rate of interest. Conversely, it is argued that the LM curve is flat because the demand for money is highly sensitive to changes in the interest rate. This comes about because relatively small changes in the interest rate can cause large changes in the speculative demand for money. Monetarists tend to discount the speculative demand which partly accounts for the difference in views.

For the following causes, state what effect each would have upon the IS and LM curve. Two have been done for you.

	Cause	Effect
1	Increase in investment	*IS curve shifts to the right*
2	Increase in demand for money	
3	Increase in consumption	
4	Decrease in investment	
5	Increase in taxation	
6	Decrease in price level	*LM curve shifts to the right*
7	Increase in government expenditure	
8	Increase in savings	
9	Increase in consumption	
10	Increase balance of payments surplus	

Rational expectations school

Criticisms of both monetarist and Keynesian theories have led to a new and controversial theory known as the 'rational expectations' or 'new classical school'. The theory maintains that individuals base their expectations on all the relevant information available to them. Such information would include economic theory, e.g. the expectations augmented Phillips curve. According to the theory, as soon as individuals see the government increase the money supply they anticipate the price inflation predicted by monetarist theory. As a result of this they immediately revise their wage and price expectations upwards. All rational policy actions of government are anticipated, so that price expectations no longer lag behind prices.

The conclusion of the theorists is that there is no scope for government moving real economic variables (such as investment) from their natural levels even in the short term. This is an extreme reversion to the economics of Smith, hence the title 'new classical'. There have been many pronouncements by ministers such as Norman Tebbit which would tend to show that they agree with this theory.

If nothing else, the new theories (IS and LM, rational expectations) present a convenient way of summarizing complex variables.

You may find it difficult to read up on these topics. An excellent summary of the new ideas is to be found in the *Economist* School Briefs which were first published in 1984.

Further reading

Hardwick, Khan and Langmead. *An Introduction to Modern Economics.* Longman. Chapters 22 and 23.
Beardshaw. *Economics: A Student's Guide.* Pitman. Chapter 36.
Vane and Thompson. *Monetarism: Theory, Evidence and Policy.* Martin Robertson. Chapters 1–3.

Once you feel confident about your knowledge of this topic try to answer the 10 multiple choice questions which follow.

Multiple choice questions

1 In the theory of portfolio balance, monetarists say that money is:

   a a substitute for a close range of financial assets.
   b an alternative to holding all other assets be they financial or physical.
   c only the high powered money stock (H) of the economy.
   d left in idle balances when interest rate are low.

answer

2 Which of the following would give the highest rate for V (velocity of circulation):

   a $\dfrac{\text{GDP}}{\text{M1}}$

   b $\dfrac{\text{NNP}}{\text{M3}}$

   c $\dfrac{\text{GDP}}{\text{M3}}$

   d $\dfrac{\text{GDP}}{\text{PSL 2}}$

answer

3 In the quantity equation of money (MV = PT), monetarists hold that:

   a V is constant.
   b V is both stable and predictable.
   c V varies directly with income.
   d changes in V can offset changes in M (the stock of money).

answer

4 Figure 4.6 demonstrates that:

   a the demand for money is erratic.
   b wage earners have a smaller demand for money but bring about a higher velocity of circulation.

c   wage earners have a greater demand for cash.

d   salaried employees stimulate a higher velocity of circulation than wage earners.

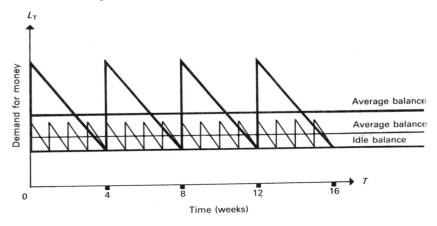

Fig. 4.6

5   It is a weakness of the quantity theory of money that:

a   there is no natural equilibrium level of national income.

b   people find inflation acceptable.

c   the price level may not respond to changes in the money stock, thereby bringing about real changes in the economy.

d   it is usually impossible to determine the value of V (velocity of circulation).

6   Which of the following is the most satisfactory definition of money in the Keynesian view of the economy? Money is:

a   anything which is readily acceptable in payment of a debt.

b   purely a means of exchange.

c   a non-interest bearing financial asset.

d   the temporary abode of purchasing power.

7   Consider the following factors:

(i) people's income
(ii) the rate of interest
(iii) expectation of changes in the rate of interest
(iv) the money supply.

Which of these, did Keynes argue, affect the demand for money:

a   (i) only?
b   (i) and (ii) only?
c   (i), (ii) and (iii) only?
d   all the items?

8   Figure 4.7 shows that:

a   increases in the money stock can be used to increase the level of national income.
b   investment is interest inelastic.
c   speculative demands for money shifts the LM curve to the right.
d   increases in the money stock leave the equilibrium of national income unchanged.

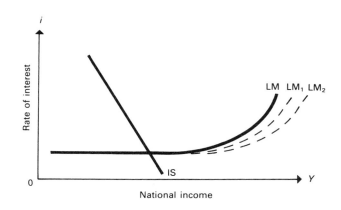

Fig. 4.7

9 The 'new classical' or 'rational expectations' theory differs from monetarism in that it holds that:

a changes in the money stock can bring about real changes in the economy.

b people will anticipate changes in the rate of inflation.

c there is a 'natural' level of unemployment.

d there is no money illusion.

 *answer*

10 The object of stating targets for monetary growth for several years ahead, as in the MTFS (medium-term financial strategy), is to:

a keep people informed.

b reduce expectations of inflation.

c reduce banks' lending.

d increase confidence in the economy.

 *answer*

 Answers follow on pages 88–92. Score 2 marks for each correct answer.

Answers

1 The correct answer is **b**.

The theory of portfolio balance is concerned with how people distribute their wealth between various assets. Friedman maintains that money is used as a medium of exchange or the temporary abode of purchasing power and is not demanded for itself. Thus people will decide how much money they need to hold and will then distribute their remaining wealth between financial assets (such as equities and bonds) and physical assets such as property. By contrast, Keynes maintained that money and financial assets could be close substitutes for one another (answer **a**).

With answer **c** we are dealing with another monetarist concept, which is Friedman and Schwartz's measure for the money supply i.e.

$$M = H \left(\frac{1 + c}{c + r} \right)$$

In answer **d** we have the Keynesian idea that when interest rates are low there will be a high speculative demand for money.

2 The correct answer is **a**.

The value of the answer will be decided by the relative sizes of the numerator and denominator. In the answer given, the GDP is the highest value for national income whereas M1 is the smallest value of the money stock given. So answer **a** must yield the highest value for V.

Three measures of V are regularly published: that for M1 (answer **a**), £M3 and M3 which are given by the formula in answer **c**. Both answers **b** and **d** would yield values for V but neither is calculated in official statistics.

3 The correct answer is **b**.

As we explained previously, in order that the quantity identity $MV \equiv PT$ can be turned into an equation, it is essential that assumptions be made about some of the components. Central to monetarist thinking about the equation is that V and T are constants. Thus, changes in the money stock (M) will lead to changes in the price level (P). Therefore if you selected answer **a** you are almost correct. However, since V does vary somewhat answer **b** is a better formulation of current monetarist thinking.

Answer **c** is incorrect. Neither monetarist nor Keynesian theory nor empirical evidence suggest that there is a simple relationship between the level of income and V. Whether or not changes in V offset changes in M (answer **d**) is debatable but it is certainly not a monetarist proposition, rather it is more extreme Keynesian than most Keynesian viewpoints today.

4 The correct answer is **b**.

You can understand the diagram by imagining peoples' wages or salary being deposited in their bank account on a weekly or monthly basis. The money is then withdrawn over a period to pay for goods and services. Of course there may be ups and downs in the demand but the diagram shows these as regular. Thus, answer **a** is incorrect.

The correct answer (**b**) envisages that if everyone was a wage earner then there would be a smaller demand for money since it would constantly be redeposited in the banking system. However, there would consequently be a high velocity of circulation. If this point is not clear, imagine what would happen if people were paid just once a year!

It follows that if answer **b** is correct then answer **c** must be wrong. It may appear tempting in that wage earners are generally less 'banked', than salary earners. From what we said in the previous paragraph it should be apparent that a switch to more salaried employment rather than wage earning would *decrease* the velocity of circulation. Therefore answer **d** is wrong.

5 The correct answer is **c**.

The question of whether or not there is a 'natural' level of equilibrium in the economy is extremely contentious. However, monetarists in general maintain that there is and, furthermore, that the equilibrium should occur at or near full employment. Therefore, answer **a** cannot be correct. With answer **b** we are confronted with a statement which is nothing to do with any theory of the economy unless it be that acceptance of inflation may breed more inflation through increased expectations.

It is generally agreed by monetarists that changes in the money stock will only lead to changes in the price level (see answer 3 in this topic). However, the inflexibility of prices (especially downwards) could mean that changes in the money stock lead to changes in the real economy — at least in the short-run. So, answer **c** is correct.

Answer **d** is clearly incorrect since values for V are regularly published by the government. It is, however, true to say that V cannot be measured, it can only be determined from the formula, i.e. in $MV = PT$ we can measure M, P and T but we can only arrive at V through application of the formula:

$$V = \frac{PT}{M}$$

6 The correct answer is **c**.

You will recall that in the Keynesian view money is a close substitute for a range of financial assets. So, we are looking for a definition which encompasses this idea. With answer **a** we have a generally accepted definition of money but one which is not specific enough to be Keynesian. Monetarists, on the other hand, see money being almost exclusively used as a means of exchange, therefore **b** might be an acceptable monetarist definition. However, Friedman maintains that people may store up money with the intention of spending in the near future. So, **d** would be a better monetarist definition of money.

This leaves us with answer **c** as an acceptable Keynesian definition. Remember that Keynes argued that people might wish to hold money as a financial asset if interest rates were low because of the speculative motive. According to this view people holding cash are doing without the interest or yield. Hence, interest bearing deposits would lie outside this view of money. This view of the money stock would correspond with the M1 measure or better still the NibM1 measure.

7 The correct answer is **c**.

According to Keynes there are three reasons why people demand money. These are the transactions, precautionary and speculative motives. The demand for money for the transactions motive is decided by peoples' income, therefore point (i) is correct. The rate of interest affects the demand for money when interest rates are high and vice versa (point (ii)). In addition to this, the demand for money will be affected by expectations of the interest rate changing. For example, a high rate of interest will cause people to speculate on a fall in interest rates and therefore demand other financial assets rather than money (point (iii)). This must, therefore, mean that response **c** is correct, although it might be argued that Keynes laid stress upon the expectations of the future rate of interest rather than the present interest rate.

If you chose answer **d** you have committed one of the cardinal errors of economics by saying that supply determines demand! Supply does not determine demand other than by influencing the price, in this case the rate of interest. It is also the case that Keynes paid little attention to the supply of money.

8 The correct answer is **d**.

The diagram shows the liquidity trap as described by Keynes. This occurs when the interest rate is so low that investment becomes totally interest elastic. This means that changes in the money stock have absolutely no effect upon the equilibrium level of national income. This being the case, answer **a** cannot be correct since this states the opposite. Answer **b** is also incorrect and is only likely to occur at high levels of interest. An increase in the speculative demand for money (answer **c**) would cause a movement along the LM curve not a shift of it.

In the diagram, the shift of the curve from LM to LM1 to LM2 would be the result of increases in the money stock but because, as you see, the lower end of the curve is horizontal; this means that this makes no difference to the intersection with the IS curve. This therefore leaves equilibrium level of income unchanged (answer **d**).

9 The correct answer is **d**.

The rational expectations school of economics is one of the newest. It is a development of monetarism and places great emphasis on the equilibrium forces in the economy. As the name implies it stresses the fact that people will act totally rationally. The question not only asks us to identify this school of thought but to distinguish it from monetarism. Quite a tall order!

Answer **a** we can dismiss since it is Keynesians who maintain that changes in the money supply can cause *real* changes in the real economy while monetarists and the new classical schools maintain that the result will only be monetary changes (at least in the long-run). Proposition **b** is not associated with any particular school of thought, although the rational expectations school would like to think that expectations of inflation can be reduced (see also MCQ 10). Both monetarists and the new classicists believe in a so called natural level of unemployment, so **c** cannot be correct.

We therefore arrive at answer **d** as the correct one. The rational expectations school maintains that people are not fooled by purely monetary changes in their income whereas monetarists believe that the monetary illusion can persist for some time. The rational expectations school is an awful lot to explain briefly but let us pass on an anecdote which is said to illustrate the fact that people are not fooled by illusory gains:

A professor of economics and a student were walking across the quadrangle when the student remarked, 'Look Professor there is a £5 note on the ground'. 'Don't be silly', replied the professor, 'if that was a £5 note someone would have picked it up'.

10 The correct answer is **b**.

Having worked through the last question you should now be familiar with the idea of rational expectations. From this arises the idea that if you state clear targets for the future for low growth of the money supply etc. it will reduce expectations of inflation thereby helping to bring this about.

Stating targets will, of course, keep people informed (answer **a**) but this is not the objective. However, the MTFS has nothing to do with either encouraging or restricting bank lending (answer **c**). Answer **d** may be an indirect result of a successful MTFS but its primary objective remains as we stated in response **b**.

Score 2 marks for each correct answer. What was your score? Fill it in on the score grid.

If you scored 12 or less and are still a bit shaky on some points go back and look at the study guide again before proceeding any further.

If you are sure you really understand and are familiar with this topic now, try the 10 further questions which are on pages 198–201. Alternatively you can go on to your next topic and do all the post-tests together at the end.

Topic 5 Monetary policy

Study guide

Monetary policy is a vast topic which lies at the heart of the subject. It is therefore essential that you understand it fully. We can divide our necessary understanding of the topic into two levels.

(i) The description of the weapons of policy, how they work and what their shortcomings are.

(ii) An appraisal of the weapons in the light of different theories, e.g. does monetary base control actually work.

You should be aware that monetary policy has changed and evolved over time. It used to be believed that changes in the rate of interest (the price of money) determined the volume of investment in the economy. Thus, lowering the rate of interest would stimulate the economy whilst raising it would contract the economy. Up to the time of the 1914–18 war, monetary policy consisted of little more than minor changes in the bank rate. The question of variation of the supply of the money supply hardly arose since the UK was on the gold standard.

Objectives of policy

The Radcliffe Report (1959) identified five objectives of monetary policy:

(i) Control of inflation
(ii) Attainment of full employment
(iii) Favourable balance of payments
(iv) Economic growth
(v) A contribution to the economies of less developed countries.

Although the report is now out of date and its policy prescriptions out of favour, the list of policy objectives remains valid. There is no disagreement about these objectives but problems arise:

* Which are the most important?
* How to achieve the objectives.

The problems are exacerbated by the fact that they often conflict with each other. For example, the conflict between full employment and the control of inflation. This is illustrated by the Phillips curve.

Whatever the objective, the main purpose of monetary policy is to regulate the level of aggregate monetary demand in the economy. We have already mentioned (see page 79) the disagreement about whether *monetary* demand affects the *real* economy.

Who operates monetary policy?

Monetary policy is ultimately in the hands of the government. But in the UK policy is implemented by the Bank of England. The Bank also has a considerable say in the formulation of policy.

In some countries, e.g. Germany and the USA, the central banks are much more independent of government than in the UK.

The stages of monetary policy

There are several links in the chain of monetary policy. For example, changes in the rate of interest have to effect investment — to effect expenditure — to promote economic growth.

> List 5 stages in the operation of monetary policy from initial instrument through to final policy objective. (You can check if you were correct in the answer to MCQ 1.)

The central link in the chain is **intermediate targets**. There are 5 of these:

    (i)   The money stock (e.g. M_1, $£M_3$ etc.)
   (ii)   Credit
 (iii)   Interest rates
 (iv)   The exchange rate
   (v)   Expenditure

In choosing which is the best or most appropriate target, the monetary authorities are constrained by two major considerations:

(i) Which target it is *possible* to control i.e. it is no good selecting a target which it is impossible to influence. Perhaps more accurately we should say that some targets are more influencable than others!

(ii) Which intermediate target is thought to influence final targets such as growth. Here there are substantial disagreements, e.g. monetarists prefer money stock and Keynesians suggest interest rates.

Exam tip: If you are taking the Easter exam (or even if you are not) make sure that you are familiar with the targets announced by the Chancellor in the budget statement.

It is a good idea to buy 2 or 3 of the heavy newspapers the day after the budget and cut out the articles. This will give you really up to date information for the exam.

Here now are a few points about each of the intermediate targets:

1 The money stock. Control of the money stock as an intermediate target is favoured by the monetarists. They believe there is a fairly direct process (transmission mechanism) through which increases in M become increases in expenditure. If the supply of money is increased people will be holding more money than they wish and will therefore buy assets including bonds. (See discussion of theory of portfolio balance on page 79.) This will increase the price of bonds and therefore decrease the rate of interest (look at page 61 if you're not sure why) thus leading to an increase in investment and therefore of expenditure generally.

The extent to which changes in the money stock affect *real* national income is a matter of fierce academic debate. (See discussion in the study guide for Topic 4.)

2 Credit. There is no necessary reason why the money stock and bank lending should change at the same rate. It is possible, for example, for banks to increase credit even if there is no increase in the money supply. It can therefore be argued that this should include not only bank credit but also credit from all other sources.

Another possibility is *selective credit control* which aims to restrict certain types of borrowing whilst permitting others.

3 Interest rates. Control of interest rates is a more Keynesian approach to monetary policy. The shortcoming of this approach is that it is difficult to demonstrate a close link between interest rates and economic activity, although high real rates in recent years have undoubtedly had adverse effects. Another problem is the extent to which the domestic government can control interest rates in the face of international pressure.

4 The exchange rate. A fall in the external value of the pound will increase the demand for exports and restrict the demand for imports. This should therefore stimulate the economy. The effect of such a change on the balance of payments is discussed in Topic 6.

Against the possible beneficial effect of a fall in the exchange rate we must balance the possible inflationary effects as the price of imports rises.

An appreciation in the exchange rate would, of course have the opposite effects to those mentioned.

For a country such as the UK which is very dependent on foreign trade the exchange rate is extremely important. The policy of the government after 1979 was largely to leave the exchange rate to the mercy of market forces, e.g. by abolishing exchange control. However, the adverse effect of large movements in the exchange rate cannot be ignored. Thus governments might be forced to intervene in currency markets by buying or selling currency or by moving interest rates.

5 Expenditure. It is possible to treat expenditure as an intermediate target of monetary policy. If treated as such, monetary policy would be adjusted in the light of growth of expenditure rather than changes in the money stock itself.

The difficulties of this approach are:

* Monetary policy takes time to work and then there is a danger of changing policy before its full effects are apparent.
* It is much more difficult to collect information on changes in expenditure quickly than it is for, say, changes in the money stock. Thus, *information lags* may pose a problem.

The weapons of policy

The issue of notes and coins

Theoretically the Bank of England could influence the volume of money by expanding or contracting the supply of cash. In practice it is very difficult for the Bank not to supply the cash which banks are demanding, so that it is not a viable method of restricting supply. The converse may not be true, indeed, many people would argue that the overprinting of bank notes, i.e. sale of government securities to the Bank's Issue Department, was one of the causes of inflation in the mid-1970s.

The introduction of a new, much narrower, definition of the money supply, termed money base (MO), consisting only of cash and banks' balances with the Bank of England, has meant that the supply of cash has assumed more importance.

Liquidity ratios

In 1981 the bank abandoned the reserve assets ratio. The only stated ratios now are the 0.5% of eligible liabilities which the monetary sector must keep with the Bank and the 5% which has to be kept with the money market. Since the Bank of England is able to influence the supply of liquid assets, it is therefore still able to influence bank lending. In addition to this, the Bank has stated that it regards the funds which the banks voluntarily retain with it for clearing purposes as 'the fulcrum for money market management'.

Interest rates

Most of the weapons of monetary policy will indirectly affect interest rates, but the Bank has a direct influence upon interest rates because the rate at which the Bank is willing to lend is crucial. Great importance used to be attached to the bank rate but this was abandoned in 1972 in favour of minimum lending rate (MLR). This was supposed to be determined by a formula geared to the Treasury bill rate, thus placing greater reliance on market forces. The announcement (or 'posting') of MLR was suspended in 1981.

The Bank now works within an unpublished band of rates. Important money market rates such as the Treasury bill rate will stay close to the Bank's lending rate. This is because the Bank's rate is kept above Treasury bill rate, so that discount houses would lose money if they are forced to borrow. Thus, all market rates tend to move in sympathy with the Bank of England's rates; clearing banks' base rate for example is always at, or near the Bank's rate.

As we mentioned at the beginning of this study guide, whether or not interest rates are an effective way of directing the economy is a matter of controversy. Monetarist thinking has tended to concentrate on the control of the money supply rather than interest rates.

It is undoubtedly true, however, that the very high real interest rates of recent years have had deleterious effects upon the economy.

Open market operations

Open market operations have long been a mysterious subject to the non-specialist student and consequently they are often neglected. However, since 1979 they have been the chief weapon of policy and it is therefore essential that you understand their operation.

Open market operations are the sale or purchase of securities by the Bank with the intention of influencing the volume of money in circulation and the rate of interest. The selling of bills or bonds should reduce the volume of money and increase interest rates, whilst the repurchase of, or reduction in sales of, government securities should increase the volume of money and increase interest rates.

In order to explain the effects of open-market operations, it is necessary to explain their effect upon the balance sheets of commercial banks. As you will see, open market operations work via the reserve, or liquid assets ratio of the bank. You could well argue that such a ratio does not exist. However, to do so would be to misunderstand the essential nature of banking business. All banks work on such a ratio. The absence of a *common ratio* for all banks should not obscure the fact that all banks are working to some ratio.

If you are at all unsure of open market operations it is essential that you work through the following example.

Example: Consider a bank whose assets and liabilities are arranged in the following manner:

1. Bank X before open-market sales

Liabilities (£)		Assets (£)	
Deposits	100,000	Liquid assets (10% ratio)	10,000
		Securities	40,000
		Advances	50,000
	£100,000		£100,000

You will note that Bank X has a liquid asset ratio of 10%. Let us now assume that the Bank of England sells securities, £1000 of which are bought by the depositors of Bank X. The customers pay for these by cheques drawn on Bank X and the Bank of England collects this money by deducting it from Bank X's balance at the Bank. So, after open-market sales, the Bank X's balance sheet will be as follows:

2. Bank X after open-market sales

Liabilities (£)		Assets (£)	
Deposits	99,000	Liquid assets (9.09% ratio)	9000
		Securities	40,000
		Advances	50,000
	£99,000		£99,000

The Bank of England's actions will have immediate (or primary) effects by reducing the amount of money in circulation by the amount of open-market sales and may also increase the interest rate if increased sales depress the price of securities. However, the most important effects of open-market operations are the secondary effects which come about as a result of Bank X's need to maintain its liquidity ratio. In order to restore its ratio the bank is forced to sell off securities, thus further reducing their price and thereby raising the rate of interest, and by reducing its advances, which may involve both making advances harder to obtain and more expensive.

3. Final position of Bank X

Liabilities (£)		Assets (£)	
Deposits	90,000	Liquid assets (10% ratio)	9000
		Securities	36,000
		Advances	45,000
	£90,000		£90,000

The final position of Bank X's balance sheet shows that in order to restore its liquidity ratio it has been forced to reduce its balance sheet to £90,000. Thus, £1000 of open-market operations have reduced the volume of money in circulation by £10,000. The magnitude of the effect is determined by the bank multiplier. If, for example, Bank X worked to a 20% ratio, then there would only be a five-fold effect.

Have you really understood this?

Go back to point 1 above and assume the balance sheet is now like this:

Bank X before open-market sales

Deposits	100,000	Liquid assets	20,000
		Securities	35,000
		Advances	45,000
	£100,000		£100,000

Note the ratio is now 20%.
Now suppose the Bank purchases securities to the value of £1000.
Work through stages 2 and 3 to show the maximum possible effect upon Bank X's balance sheet.

Did you end up with a final balance of £105,000? If not try again.

Funding

Converting short-term government debt (such as Treasury bills) into longer-term debt (such as Exchequer bonds) is called funding. This will not only reduce liquidity but also, if the Bank of England is replacing securities which could be counted as liquid assets by securities which cannot, it could bring about the multiple contraction of deposits described above. In recent years the government has been concerned to borrow money in a way which would not increase banks' supplies of liquid assets and has therefore created more longer-term non-negotiable securities such as 'granny bonds'. If the authorities convert (fund) more government debt than the borrowing requirement for the year (PSBR) this is known as *overfunding*.

Special directives and special deposits

If the Bank calls upon the members of the monetary sector to make a deposit of a certain percentage of their liabilities in cash at the Bank, and stipulates that these may not be counted as liquid assets, then this brings about the multiple contraction of their lending in the same way as open-market operations, the difference being that it is more certain and less expensive. The power to call for special deposits was specifically retained in the monetary control-provisions of 1981.

The Bank of England has issued special directives on both how banks should lend (quantitative) and to whom they should lend (qualitative). However, since the competition and credit control changes of 1971 it has ceased to make quantitative directives and makes only qualitative ones.

The corset

In 1973 a new scheme termed supplementary special deposits and nicknamed 'the corset' came into operation. By this scheme, if banks expanded their interest-bearing eligible liabilities (IBELS) too quickly they automatically had to make special deposits of cash with the Bank. The scheme was abandoned in 1980.

Problems affecting the efficacy of the weapons of policy

We have already mentioned the dispute concerning the efficacy of interest rates. Other weapons depend upon affecting the liquidity of banks. If, however, banks keep surplus liquidity this will protect them against such measures as open-market operations and special deposits. The more liquid the assets which banks possess, the less they will be affected by policy changes; for example, an increase in the interest rate from 9 to 10% would reduce the value of securities with 3 months to run by less than 0.25 per cent, whilst long-dated stock would have its value cut by anything up to 15%.

The efficacy of open-market sales is also affected by who purchases the securities.

In order for open-market sales to be effective, it is necessary that sales be made to the general public. If the securities are bought by the banks they will have little effect upon their liquidity since most of them count as liquid assets.

When we consider special deposits and special directives we discover that these can be simple, cheap, effective and quick acting. However, in recent years governments have tried to avoid using them because they tend to damage the relationship between the central bank and the commercial banks. They also have the effect of distorting market forces. So, government policy now tends to concentrate upon manipulating market forces rather than imposing its will directly on the system.

The development of monetary policy

Policy in 1950s and 1960s

This era has been named the age of 'stop-go' policies. In the 'go' phase the government would expand the economy to stimulate output and raise economic growth. But the higher level of demand and economic activity would sooner or later suck in more imports and cause a deficit on the balance of payments. Since the UK was committed to a regime of fixed exchange rates, this problem could not be solved by devaluing the currency. In order to deal with the balance of payments deficit the government had to reduce the level of economic activity, so as to decrease imports and encourage more exports (the 'stop' phase). Then, when the balance of payments problem had disappeared, economic expansion could begin again.

This approach to economic policy meant that the government was always actively seeking to manage the level of demand in the economy. The main method of **demand management** was fiscal policy. When the government wished to expand demand it would increase public expenditure and/or lower taxes. During this period it was generally believed that fiscal policy was a more reliable way of managing, or steering, the economy than monetary policy. The main reason for this was that changes in interest rates were not thought to have very much effect on investment or other types of expenditure. However it came to be believed that raising interest rates would 'lock-up' investment funds in financial institutions. This was because a large proportion of their assets were in government securities and a rise in interest rates would decrease their value, therefore making institutions unwilling to sell them because they would make a loss. So the orthodox view at this time was that putting up rates would 'choke off' investment and was therefore useful in restricting the economy. Conversely, lowering interest rates would not, of itself, be sufficient to stimulate the econom.

The Radcliffe Report (Committee on the Working of the Monetary

System, 1959), endorsing the view that the control of overall liquidity was more important than control of the money supply, said:

> We advocate measures to strike more directly and rapidly at the liquidity of spenders. We regard a combination of the control of capital issues, bank advances and consumer credit as being most likely to serve this purpose.

The Report was subsequently criticised for its lack of attention to control of the money supply. The Report argued that any contrived changes in the money supply was as likely as not to be offset by changes in the velocity of circulation. This view was also challenged by monetarists in later years.

The Radcliffe Report's conclusions formed the basis of government monetary policy in the 1960s and early 1970s. In particular, it was believed that monetary policy should be concerned with the fine tuning of the economy, whilst its overall direction was a matter of fiscal policy.

The rise in monetarist ideas

The competition and credit control regulations of 1971 (CCC) were an important change in policy. From this date interest rates were supposed to be left free to be determined by market forces. Competition was to be encouraged by such measures as the abolition of the syndicated bid for Treasury bills and the abandonment of the clearing banks' cartel on interest rates. The CCC changes also abandoned the old 28% liquid assets ratio in favour of a 12½% reserve assets ratio. This resulted in an unprecedented rise in the money supply which was one of the major causes of inflation in subsequent years.

Monetarist economists in the UK and the USA were convinced that the only way to control inflation was through control of the money supply. The increasing severity of inflation and the apparent inability of traditional fiscal and incomes policy methods to deal with it won many people over to the monetarist school. In particular the IMF was convinced of the need to control M. Thus when the UK was forced to apply for a major loan in 1976 it was only granted it on the condition that the money supply be controlled. The accession of monetarist ideas to dominance in monetary policy can be seen to date from 1976.

In 1979 a Conservative government was elected which placed control of the money supply at the centre of its policies. From this date monetary policy was believed to be pre-eminent, with fiscal policy taking a back seat.

The medium term financial strategy

In the previous section of the study guide we mentioned the importance expectations in determining inflation. It was believed that one way of reducing expectations and therefore inflation was to announce firm targets for growth of the money stock and this practice was started in 1976. From 1976 until 1981 targets were announced for only one monetary aggregate, sterling M3.

Though the targets for the rate of growth of sterling M_3 were gradually reduced over the years, these targets were often exceeded. The reasons for this included the difficulty of estimating the demand for bank lending, the fact that other objectives were sometimes given priority over monetary control, and special factors which have sometimes boosted the money stock. In 1980 the government introduced the **medium-term financial strategy** (MTFS), which set out plans for monetary, public spending and tax policies for a number of years ahead. The basic aims of the MTFS have been to reduce inflation and to transfer more resources to the private sector.

Since this date indicators other than M3 have been added. The difficulty of controlling M3 caused it to be dropped as an aim of policy in 1985 and greater emphasis was placed on monetary base control.

Monetary base control

Under this approach, the central bank closely regulates the commercial banks' deposits (or balances) with itself. Banks need to hold balances at the central bank since it is by transferring these balances that the banks make payments between themselves and also to the government; also it is by drawing on these balances that the banks can obtain more cash to meet withdrawals of cash by their customers. Because the banks need to hold balances with the central bank, it may be possible to control the growth of the banks' lending and deposits by limiting the amount of these balances that are available to the banks. The balances which banks hold, together with cash in circulation, correspond with the money base (M_0) measure of money. Hence controlling the money supply in this way is known as monetary base control.

Conclusion

The primacy of monetary policy seems assured so long as control of inflation remains the chief objective of policy. However a greater emphasis on other objectives of policy, such as control of unemployment may see alternative policy measures such as fiscal, or even prices and incomes policy returning to prominence and lead to changes in monetary policy.

Further reading

Make sure you keep up to date with developments by reading newspapers etc.

Brown. *A Guide to Monetary Policy*. Banking Information Service. This is only 70 pages long and therefore you should be familiar with all of it.

Prest and Coppock. *The UK Economy* 9th edn. Weidenfeld & Nicolson. Chapter 2.

Griffiths and Wall. *Applied Economics*. Longman. Chapter 16.

Vane and Thompson. *Monetarism: Theory, Evidence and Policy*. Martin Robertson. Chapter 5.

Once you feel confident about your knowledge of this topic try to answer the 10 multiple choice questions which follow.

Multiple choice questions

1   The purpose of monetary policy is to achieve overall policy objectives, such as the control of inflation. To achieve this policy progresses through a number of stages. Consider the following list of policy stages and then place them in the correct order from start to finish:
   (i)   Operating policy targets
   (ii) Instruments of policy
   (iii) Actual effect on aggregate demand
   (iv) Intermediate policy targets

   The correct order is:

   a   (i) (ii) (iv) (iii).
   b   (ii) (i) (iv) (iii).
   c   (ii) (iv) (iii) (i).
   d   (iii) (ii) (i) (iv).

   answer

2   Fiscal policy is likely to interact with monetary policy in that:

   a   budget deficits affect the PSBR and thereby the money supply.
   b   changes in government borrowing will affect the price of gilt edged securities and thus affect the rate of interest.
   c   a reduction in government expenditure is likely to lead to a slower growth in the money supply.
   d   all of these.

   answer

3   Consider the following hypothetical figures for 198X. As a result of these figures what should be the change in £M3.

	£m
PSBR	12,800
Sales of public sector debt to non-bank private sector	13,300
Increase in bank lending in sterling to private and overseas sector	13,400
Net external inflow (+) to private sector	200
Increase in banks' non deposit liabilities	2000
	£ m.

£M3 would increase by:

a   £41,700m.
b   £28,400m.
c   £11,100m.
d   £ 9110m.

answer

4   If the Bank of England were to undertake open market sales of securities of £5m this would immediately reduce the volume of commercial bank deposits with the Bank of England by £5m. Supposing that the banking sector was working on a reserve requirement of 5%, then what would be the maximum possible *additional* contraction in the money supply which could result from banks adjusting their assets and liabilities to maintain the ratio. Is it:

a   £100m?
b   £ 95m?
c   £ 20m?
d   £ 15m?

answer

5   Which of the following is the most likely result of an increase in interest rates:

a   a decrease in the cost of public borrowing?
b   discouragement of overseas investment in sterling?
c   a fall in the sales of gilts?
d   a fall in tax income from the industrial sector?

answer

6   When MLR was introduced in 1972 it was intended that it should be:

a   determined by the Bank of England.
b   decided by the government.
c   determined by market forces.
d   independent of the short-term dictates of monetary policy.

answer

7   The expression 'base drift' may be used to explain the process by which:

   a   the tendency of targets for monetary base have to be constantly revised.

   b   the exceeding of a monetary target in one year will cause subsequent years targets to be correspondingly higher than intended.

   c   banks keep surplus liquidity above the requirements of the regulatory authorities, thus protecting themselves from monetary control by the authorities.

   d   the wide monetary base of the economy (M0) has constantly increased.

 *answer*

8   The expression 'overfunding' is used to describe the process by which:

   a   longer-term government securities are substituted for shorter-term in order to reduce the liquidity of the system.

   b   application for government funds are often oversubscribed.

   c   banks frequently keep excess liquidity to guard against contractionary monetary measures of the Bank of England.

   d   public sector debt in excess of the governments' needs is sold to the non-bank private sector to restrict the growth in the money supply.

 *answer*

9   Which of the following reserve requirements was in force following the Monetary control-provisions of 1981:

   a   12½% reserve assets ratio?

   b   1½% cash deposits with the Bank of England?

   c   4% of liabilities to be held with the LDMA?

   d   8% cash ratio?

 *answer*

10   According to the monetarists school of thought, in order for monetary base control to be effective it is necessary that the Bank of England:

a limits the issue of notes.
b controls short-term interest rates.
c sets firm targets for monetary growth.
d ceases to act as lender of last resort.

 _answer_

 Answers follow on pages 109–113. Score 2 marks for each correct answer.

Answers

1 The correct answer is **b**.

This is simply a matter of understanding what the expressions mean and then placing them in the correct time sequence.

First *Instruments of policy* (ii) which include, for example, open market operations or special deposits which the Bank of England uses to implement policy. It will take some time before these begin to act upon:

Operating policy targets (i) such as the liquidity of banks. These in turn will affect such things as the growth of the money stock which are termed:

Intermediate targets (iv). They are termed 'intermediate' because they are not the actual objective of policy but are important steps along the way. For example, restricting the money supply is seen as essential in achieving the overall policy objective of controlling inflation. To do this they must affect:

Aggregate demand (iii). This is the actual level of national income as measured by GDP, NNP etc. The control of which leads directly to the ultimate policy objective.

2 The correct answer is **d**.

This answer is a bit sneaky since, as experienced 'A' levellers will know, it is a good rule of thumb to avoid answers which say 'all of these'.

In the days of Keynesian demand management (1945–1970) fiscal policy was seen as most important with monetary policy being concerned with the 'fine tuning' of the economy. This position is now reversed. An extreme monetarists' view would see fiscal policy as important only in so far as it affects monetary policy and the only important prescription for fiscal policy — the reduction of government expenditure.

Let us consider the other answers. A budget deficit (answer **a**), be it increased or decreased, is very likely to affect the size of the PSBR and as you can see in the answer to the next question PSBR is a major ifluence of the change in the size of £M3. Increased government borrowing would decrease the price of securities and thereby raise the rate of interest and vice versa. Thus, answer **b** is correct. Answer **c** is also correct since a reduction in government expenditure is likely to lead to a decreased PSBR and this leads to a slower growth in £M3.

3 The correct answer is **c**.

This is a very exacting question and so if you did not find the correct answer don't be too hard on yourself. However, it is essential that you do understand what causes changes in the various measures of money stock.

In the question it is simply a matter of knowing what to add on to £M3 and what to take away. All of the other answers result from getting the + or − signs wrong.

The following is the correct sequence:

Plus	PSBR
Minus	sales of public debt to non-bank private sector
Plus	increase in sterling lending
Plus or Minus	net external flow of sterling to private sector (in this case we are told it is plus)
Minus	Increase in non-deposit liabilities (such as share capital etc.)

If you do not follow this then re-read the chapters on definitions of the money supply.

Note In these figures 'overfunding' has taken place. See question 8 in this section.

4   The correct answer is **b**.

If you do not understand the answer to this then you must turn to the study guide and go through the section on *open market operations*.

If the banks are working on a reserve ratio of 5% then there will be a bank multiplier of 20. Thus, the possible expansion or contraction of bank deposits as a result of open market operations of £5m would be £100m. So the immediate reduction in the money stock of £5m will be followed up by a further possible reduction of up to £95m.

It is entirely possible, of course, that open market operations may not be this effective. Remember their efficacy will be affected by:
* how near banks are to their liquid assets ratio
* who buys the securities sold by the bank

The absence of one uniform ratio in the modern monetary sector makes calculation more difficult.

5   The correct answer is **d**.

The explanation for the correct answer is rather tricky but it should be obvious that the other answers are incorrect. It is clear that a rise in the interest rates will increase the cost of public borrowing so answer **a** must be incorrect. Higher interest rates will encourage overseas investors to invest their money in sterling and so answer **b** is also incorrect. Similarly increased interest rates are likely to encourage people to buy gilt edged securities provided that further rises are not expected (answer **c**).

We are thus left with answer **d** which we can explain as follows: Increased interest rates will almost certainly lead to decreased profits for companies and government tax revenues from taxes on company profits will fall.

6 The correct answer is **c**.

Prior to the introduction of MLR in 1972 the Bank of England used to announce the Bank Rate weekly. The Bank Rate could be defined as the minimum rate at which the Bank was willing to lend or rediscount bills of exchange, i.e. act as lender of last resort. This situation is covered by answer **a**. If answer **a** is incorrect then clearly answer **b** is also. Much as we may see MLR and Bank Rate as being decided by the Bank and/or the government it was the intention in 1972 that the rate be fixed by market forces. A formula was arrived at which linked MLR to Treasury bill rate. MLR was to be 2½% above TBR rounded to the nearest ¼%. However the Bank was soon forced to intervene and by 1978 had abandoned all pretence of an independent market rate. Since the suspension of MLR in 1981 the Bank has once again returned to the idea of manipulating market rates.

Answer **d** might at first glance appear to be correct in light of the above explanation. But the fact that MLR may have been fixed by market forces did not mean that the government did not manipulate interest rates through open market operations etc. It is never possible for the interest rate to be independent of monetary policy. (See also answer to question 10.)

7 The correct answer is **b**.

Here again we have a question where all the other responses are also true but relate to other circumstances. Answer **a** is true — Monetary targets are constantly being revised because of overshoot but this is not called base drift even though it may be connected with it.

Banks do often keep surplus liquidity (answer **c**) to protect themselves from Bank of England policies. But this is nothing to do with base drift. Incidently, reserve requirements are *not* statutory as suggested in the question. They are regulations laid down by the Bank.

Wide monetary base Mo has constantly increased (answer **d**) but this is simply the expansion of money supply and not base drift.

The government sets targets for money base, e.g. it may suggest that it increases by no more than 10% per year. If, however, in year one it increases by 15% then in year two a growth of 10% would result in an overall growth in the money base of 26.5% over the 2 years instead of 21% (remember it is a compound rate). This is known as base drift. If overshoot does occur the government will be faced with the problem of whether or not to redefine the targets.

8 The correct answer is **d**.

Answer **a** describes the process of 'funding' not 'overfunding'. A funding operation has the effect of deliquifying the system and thus has a contractionary effect on the money supply. It has the disadvantage, however, that it raises interest rates.

There is no particular expression for the oversubscription of government stock (answer **b**). We have already mentioned the fact that banks frequently keep excess liquidity (answer **c**) to protect themselves from monetary policy. This again is not overfunding.

Overfunding is correctly defined in answer **d**. It is a policy to offset the effect of rising bank lending on the money stock. It is associated with the 'bill mountain' and was mentioned in the Chancellor's autumn statement in 1985.

9 The correct answer is **c**.

You really should have got this one right because the other responses clearly apply to other periods. The 12½% reserve assets ratio (RAR) was the system in operation from 1971–1981. This is also true of the 1½% cash deposit referred to in answer **b**. The 8% cash ratio was abolished in 1971!

Since 1981 eligible banks have been obliged to keep a certain amount of money with the London Discount Houses Association. Originally this was 4% but this was later reduced to 2½%. Thus answer **c** is correct.

10 The correct answer is **d**.

You will have to understand monetarist thinking very well indeed to answer this question. If you got it right you can justly feel proud of yourself.

Let us consider the other responses — all of which seem reasonable. The limitation of the issue of notes (answer **a**) may seem reasonable but in practice it is very difficult to limit the issue of notes. The Bank of England is obliged to provide the banks with the notes they require. It is unthinkable that the Bank could refuse to issue notes to the banks.

Monetary policy prescriptions concentrate on controlling the supply of money and letting the interest rate sort itself out. Thus, answer **b** is the wrong way round. Answer **c** is associated with monetarism or more particularly the rational expectations school but monetary targets are usually set by the government not by the Bank of England. Also setting targets has little to do with making monetary policy effective.

If a government is wedded to the idea of strict control of the money supply it follows that it cannot simultaneously control the price of money i.e. the rate of interest. The lender of last resort function ensures that in the event of a cash shortage the central bank is always willing to provide liquidity. This means that the bank is rescued from the consequences of the lack of cash generated by the control of the money supply. So, if monetary control is to be effective it is therefore necessary for the central bank to abandon its lender of last resort function (answer **d**).

Score 2 marks for each correct answer. What was your score? Fill it in on the score grid.

If you scored 12 or less and are still a bit shaky on some points go back and look at the study guide again before proceeding any further.

If you are sure you really understand and are familiar with this topic now, try the 10 further questions which are on pages 202–204. Alternatively you can go on to your next topic and do all the post-tests together at the end.

Topic 6   Balance of payments

Study guide

The level of knowledge required for the exam varies quite significantly from topic to topic. With the balance of payments we have a topic which is usually treated in a straightforward manner. It is therefore a good topic to revise thoroughly.

Defining the balance

The balance of payments is an account of all the transactions of everyone living and working in the UK with the rest of the world.

If a person normally resident in the UK sells goods or services to someone abroad, this creates an inflow (+) of money, whilst anyone in the UK buying goods or services abroad creates an outflow (−), whilst if a foreigner invests in the UK, e.g. if a US company takes over a UK company, then an inflow (+) of currency is created. Not so obviously, if the UK reduces its reserves of foreign currency, this is recorded as a credit (+), as is the receipt of loans from abroad, whilst, conversely, increasing the reserves of foreign currency, or making a loan is shown as a debit (−). When all these transactions are recorded we arrive at a balance of payments statement as in Table 6.1.

Items in the account

The numbers against the following headings refer to items in Table 1.

1 Current account. This has two main components: visible trade, which is the export and import of goods (from which we get the balance of trade); and invisible trade, which is the sale and purchase of services. The balance of trade is often confused with the balance of payments as you can see from Table 1 it is only a part of the balance of payments, albeit an important part. It is therefore possible to have a deficit on the balance of trade but a surplus on the balance of payments, or vice versa. The traditional pattern for the UK is to have a deficit on the balance of trade made up by a surplus on invisibles. However the advent of North

Table 6.1 Balance of payments of the UK 1984

Item	£m.
Current account	
Visible trade:	
Exports (FOB)	70,409
Imports (FOB)	74,510
Visible balance (balance of trade)	−4,101
Invisibles	
General government	−923
Private sector,	
Sea transport	−1,151
Civil aviation	469
Travel	−448
Financial and other services	6,038
Interest profit and dividends	
General government	−2,282
Private sector	4,586
Transfers	−2,253
Invisible balance	5,036
Current account balance (1)	935
Investment and other capital transactions (2)	−3,291
Balancing item (3)	+1,040
Balance for official financing, (4)	−1,316
Made up as follows:	
Current balance	935
Investment and capital transactions	3,291
Balancing item	+1,040
Official financing, financed as follows	
IMF	—
Other monetary authorities	—
Foreign currency borrowing	+408
Changes in official reserves (drawings on (+)/addition to (−)	+908
Total official financing (5)	+1,316

Sea oil has altered this and at the present time, there is often a surplus. Other changes in the current account involve the growing propensity to import manufactured goods and the decline in the relative size of the invisible surplus.

2 Investment and other capital transactions. This involves the movement of capital (money) rather than goods or services, i.e. it is concerned with international loans (not currency loans) and investment. It includes such items as:

* government loans to foreign countries
* overseas investment in the UK
* UK investment overseas
* borrowing and lending overseas by UK and foreign banks

This part of the account is often a deficit. Its importance has grown in recent years, as has its instability. This instability is caused by large movements of short-term capital. This so-called 'hot money' tends to move about in search of better interest rates or expectations of changes in the value of currencies.

3 The balancing item. This item is necessary to allow for statistical errors in the compilation of the account. It can be either positive or negative. Old accounts are often adjusted in the light of better information and, for this reason, the size of the balancing item may be made smaller.

4 The balance for official financing (total currency flow). This is the net flow of currency which results from all the country's external transactions. It is the result of the aggregate of the balance from current account, investment and other capital transactions and the balancing item. This is the balance of the balance of payments. In Table 6.1 it is £1316m, i.e. there was an overall deficit.

5 Official financing. In the short-term any overall deficit or surplus is balanced by official financing. In the event of a deficit, the government would cope with it by running down reserves of foreign currency or by borrowing foreign currency from international organisations such as the IMF or from foreign currency banks. Thus, as you can see in Table 6.1, a surplus (+) has been created in this account exactly equal to the deficit (−). Conversely an overall surplus on the balance of payments would be balanced by the government increasing its reserves of foreign currency or making loans or reducing its debts to foreign countries.

The figures in Table 6.2 are taken from the annual balance of payments statement of Pacifica. Prepare:

(1) Pacifica's balance of payments statement to show the balance of visible trade, the invisible balance, the balance on current account, the balance for official financing, official financing and the balancing item.

(2) This task is based on an actual IoB question. As you can

see, it is very straightforward if you can work the mechanics of balance of payments. The question went on to ask whether the figures suggested that Pacifica was a developed or underdeveloped country. Check that you understand this part by listing at least four points which suggest the state of Pacifica's economy.

If you are in difficulty, some guidance is given on page 123.

Table 6.2 Pacifica's balance of payments

Item	$m.
Capital transactions	−750
Banking earnings	+1200
Insurance earnings	+500
Interest paid abroad	−300
Interest received from abroad	+900
Exports of manufactures (FOB)	+18,000
Exports of raw materials and fuel (FOB)	+8,000
Imports of manufactures (CIF)	−15,000
Imports of raw materials and fuel (CIF)	−14,000
Shipping earnings (net)	+250
Tourist earnings	+500
Change in reserves	−1200

Why the balance always balances

It is often said that 'the balance of payments always balances'. This is indeed true, both in the short term and the long term. In the short term, as we have seen above, a balance is achieved through official financing so that any disequilibrium is adjusted through changes in reserves and loans. In the long term we can also demonstrate that a balance will be arrived at because, if there is any deficit on the current account, this must be matched by a surplus on investment and other capital transactions or else by a surplus in future years to pay back borrowing etc. The fact that a balance must eventually be achieved may, however, obscure the fact that a disequilibrium exists in the short term. A short-term disequilibrium need not change major problems as it may be conveniently dealt with by a change in reserves or by borrowing or lending. A long-term or fundamental disequilibrium exists when there is a persistent tendency for outflows of trade and capital to be significantly greater or smaller than the corresponding inflows.

117

Problems and solutions

In the case of a disequilibrium the correct policy on solution will depend upon:
— whether it is a deficit or surplus
— the size of the problem
— the cause of the problem
— the exchange rate regime in force

Figure 6.1 summarizes some of the possible combinations of problems. A deficit on the balance of payments might be accompanied by either a high or low level of domestic activity. The required solutions would obviously be very different; for example, if an external deficit was accompanied by heavy unemployment domestically, a solution which aimed at further depressing the level of economic activity would hardly be ideal. Similarly, when we consider the possibility of a surplus on the

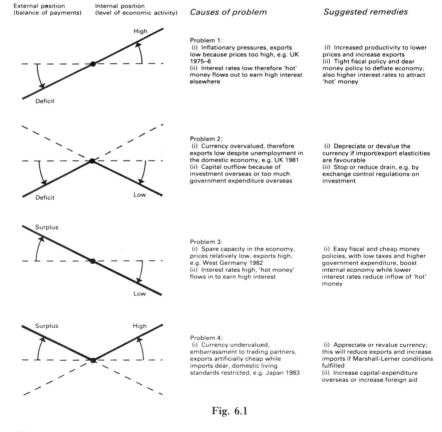

External position (balance of payments)	Internal position (level of economic activity)	Causes of problem	Suggested remedies
Deficit	High	**Problem 1:** (i) Inflationary pressures, exports low because prices too high, e.g. UK 1975–6 (ii) Interest rates low therefore 'hot' money flows out to earn high interest elsewhere	(i) Increased productivity to lower prices and increase exports (ii) Tight fiscal policy and dear money policy to deflate economy; also higher interest rates to attract 'hot' money
Deficit	Low	**Problem 2:** (i) Currency overvalued, therefore exports low despite unemployment in the domestic economy, e.g. UK 1981 (ii) Capital outflow because of investment overseas or too much government expenditure overseas	(i) Depreciate or devalue the currency if import/export elasticities are favourable (ii) Stop or reduce drain, e.g. by exchange control regulations on investment
Surplus	Low	**Problem 3:** (i) Spare capacity in the economy, prices relatively low, exports high, e.g. West Germany 1982 (ii) Interest rates high, 'hot money' flows in to earn high interest	(i) Easy fiscal and cheap money policies, with low taxes and higher government expenditure, boost internal economy while lower interest rates reduce inflow of 'hot' money
Surplus	High	**Problem 4:** (i) Currency undervalued, embarrassment to trading partners, exports artificially cheap while imports dear, domestic living standards restricted, e.g. Japan 1983	(i) Appreciate or revalue currency; this will reduce exports and increase imports if Marshall-Lerner conditions fulfilled (ii) Increase capital-expenditure overseas or increase foreign aid

Fig. 6.1

balance of payments, this too could be accompanied by either a high or low level of domestic activity.

The type of exchange rate policy to which a country is committed will also influence the situation. When the country is committed to fixed exchange rates this limits the options. This was the case in the UK up to 1972. Under these circumstances the UK was often obliged to subordinate internal policy, such as the pursuit of economic growth, to the external objective of maintaining the exchange rate. However, the option of a floating exchange rate has still not entirely freed internal policy from external constraints.

Surplus problems

It may not be apparent that a surplus is a problem. However, the following points should be considered:

(a) **Embarrassment to one's trading partners.** This may lead to a deteriorization of internal relations.

(b) **De-industrialization.** The UK's experience of surplus in the late 1970s and early 1980s has demonstrated that a surplus can lead to undesirable domestic consequences. The oil surplus were used to finance industrial imports, thereby leading to an erosion of the manufacturing base of the economy.

(c) **Feedback effects.** Since overall the international balance of payments of all trading nations must balance, then a surplus in one country causes a deficit in another. The deficit country will be forced to rectify the situation and move back into surplus thus re-exporting (or feeding back) the deficit of the previously surplus nation.

(d) **Inflationary consequences.** Both Keynesian and monetarist analysis of a balance of payments surplus points to possible inflationary consequences. In Keynesian analysis demand-pull inflation will be caused if the economy is at, or near, full employment since a surplus is an injection into the economy. Monetarists argue that a surplus increases the money supply unless exchange rates are freely floating.

Deficit problems

Rectification policies can be divided into two categories:

(a) **Expenditure reducing.** These are measures such as domestic deflation which aim to rectify the deficit by cutting expenditure.

(b) **Expenditure switching.** This refers to measures such as import controls, designed to switch expenditure from imports to domestically produced goods.

The two types of measures need not be regarded as alternatives but rather as *complements*; for example, a government might reduce expenditure to create spare capacity in the economy prior to creating extra demand through expenditure-switching policies.

Possible measures

1 Deflation. Deflationary policies are used (*expenditure reducing*) to restrict the level of aggregate demand, thereby reducing the level of imports. This may appear a rather roundabout method but a country may use this method because:
* it wishes to retain a fixed exchange rate
* other measures may conflict with treaty obligations such as GATT
* protective measures such as import controls may invite retaliation from trading partners.

Deflation was the chief method of rectifying deficits in the UK in the period 1945–67.

Deflation might have a secondary expenditure-switching effect if domestic rates of inflation are reduced below those of the nation's trading partners, thus giving it a price advantage.

2 Protection. Protective measures include:
* Tariffs
* Quotas
* Non tariffs barriers (such as complicated safety regulations)
* Exchange control regulations.

Name 4 protective measures. Number 1 is done for you.
1. The EEC variable import levy on the import of foodstuffs produced outside the EEC.

Protective measures are *expenditure switching*. They will probably do nothing about the underlying causes of the deficit rather they attempt to cure it by cutting off imports.

3 Devaluation or depreciation. If a nation operating a fixed exchange rate drops the price of its currency, this is referred to as *devaluation*. If a country has a 'floating' exchange rate and it allows the external value of its currency to decrease, this is referred to as *depreciation*. Both of these actions have the same effect i.e. exports will become cheaper to foreigners whilst imports will be more expensive to domestic consumers. These measures are thus *expenditure switching*.

4 Other measures. We have considered the usual measures for rectifying payments deficits. In short-term the deficit could be cured simply by *borrowing* or *reducing reserves*. A nation such as the UK might also consider reducing *military expenditure overseas* or reducing *foreign* *aid.* Alternatively it might *restrict the outflow or capital* or *encourage inward investment.*

Some other problems

1 The J-curve. It is frequently the case that measures taken to rectify a balance of payments deficit have often led to an immediate deterioration in the payments position followed by a subsequent recovery. This gives rise to the so-called J-curve. This is more fully explained in the answer to MCQ 6.

2 The Marshall–Lerner criterion. The efficiency of devaluation or depreciation as a method of rectifying a deficit is determined by the Marshall–Lerner criterion.

A.P. Lerner in his book 'Economics of Control' applied Alfred Marshall's ideas on elasticity to foreign trade. It is clear that devaluation will increase total earnings from exports ony if demand for exports is elastic and, similarly, expenditure on imports will only be reduced by devaluation if demand for imports is elastic. However, the question arises as to how the relative elasticities of demand affect the balance of payments position. The Marshall–Lerner criterion states that devaluation will only improve the balance of payments if the sum of the elasticities of demand for exports and imports is greater than unity. Conversely, a payment surplus would be reduced by revaluation if the same criterion was fulfilled. (See short answer question 3, p.5.)

3 The terms of trade. The current account of the Balance of Payments can be affected by the terms of trade which is a measure of the relative prices of imports and exports. It is calculated by taking the index of export prices and dividing it by the index of import prices. The index is completed from a sample of the prices of 200 commodities whilst the export index samples 250.

The present index is based on 1980. If, for example, we find that in 1985 the index of export prices was 135 whilst that for imports was 131, we can then calculate the terms of trade as:

$$\text{Terms of trade} = \frac{\text{Index of export prices}}{\text{Index of import prices}} \times \frac{100}{1}$$

$$= \frac{135}{131} \times \frac{100}{1}$$

$$= \underline{103}$$

If the index increases this is said to be a *favourable* movement in the terms of trade, whilst when it falls it is termed *unfavourable*. A favourable movement in the terms of trade means that a given quantity of exports will buy more imports. The word favourably may, however, be misleading; a relative rise in the price of exports will only be beneficial if the demand for exports is inelastic.

See also the comments on the Marshall-Lerner criterion.

Return to the balance of payments statement at the beginning of this unit and work your way through all the items in the current account. In each case say what you think would happen in the case of a significant depreciation of the currency.

Was your answer borne out during the period of depreciation 1982–85?

If not why not?

Keynesian and monetarist views

The **Keynesian approach** to the balance of payments would look on it in terms of whether aggregate demand is sufficient to absorb national output. We write the equilibrium condition for the economy as:

$$Y = C + I + G + (X - M)$$

You can write this as:

$$X - M = Y - (C + I + G)$$

The lefthandside of the equation $(X - M)$ shows the overall payments deficit or surplus. On the other side the expression $C + I + G$ is an identity known as total domestic expenditure (TDE). Whilst on the other side we have Y which may be identified with GDP. From this we can see that the balance of payments will be in deficit if total domestic expenditure is greater than GDP.

From this we can argue that devaluation or depreciation of the currency will only be successful if TDE does not absorb the whole of GDP. For this condition to be fulfilled, there must be spare capacity in the economy, otherwise output will not be able to rise to meet the increased demand for exports.

We must now consider the income effect that any depreciation of the currency might have. Any increase in value of exports which is induced will, via the multiplier, create an increase in national income which will in turn create more demand for imports. Thus, even if there is spare capacity in the economy, absorbtion will reduce the effect of any depreciation.

The absorbtion approach underlines the necessity to have spare capacity in the economy before attempting a depreciation of the currency, demonstrating that it may be necessary to undertake expenditure-reducing policies before expenditure-switching depreciation.

The need to combat inflationary pressure created by rising import prices may also argue for the necessity to control factor incomes, for example by an incomes policy.

This Keynesian approach to the balance of payments concentrates on the current account. Therefore, if the problem lies with the capital account other measures will have to be taken such as exchange control.

The **monetarist approach** to the balance of payments lays stress upon the type of exchange rate regime which is in force. If a country is on a fixed exchange rate, a deficit will cause an expansion of the money supply because the government will be forced to buy up its currency on foreign exchange markets to prevent the exchange rate falling. A surplus would have the opposite effect. However, with a floating exchange rate any imbalance would be adjusted by appreciation or depreciation of the currency. Since monetarists place great emphasis on the control of the money supply, it is easy to see why they favour floating exchange rates.

However, it would be more strictly monetarist if we approach the payments position from the point of view of how changes in the money supply affect the balance of payments. The monetarists view is that the balance of payments is a monetary problem. The economy will be in equilibrium if the total demand for money (L) is equal to the total supply (M). The supply of money, however, is the result of that which is created domestically plus any net inflow resulting from a payments surplus or minus any outflow resulting from a deficit. According to this view, a too-rapid increase of the money supply will cause a payments deficit because the supply of money will exceed the demand. Thus, if a country wishes to maintain its payments equilibrium it must control its money supply. Hence, a monetarist prescription for a stable balance of payments situation would be one in which there is a regime of floating exchange coupled with tight control of the money supply.

 Since the Keynesian view only appears to be concerned with the current account does this make the monetarist view more acceptable? (See the pros and cons of fixed and fluctuating exchange rates in the next unit.)

Guidance on exercise on page 117
   (1) You should have arrived at a balance for official financing of (−)1200 and a balancing item of (−)500.
   (2) Pacifica is obviously a developed country as is evidenced by large banking earnings, interest received from abroad, large amounts of manufactured exports, capital exported etc.

Further reading

Pratt, M.J. *A Guide to the International Financial System.* Banking Information Services. Chapter 2.

Carter and Partington. *Applied Economics in Banking and Finance.* Oxford University Press. Chapter 11.

Prest and Coppock. *The UK Economy* 9th edn. Weidenfeld & Nicolson. Chapter 3.

Preston, M.H. *The British Economy.* Philip Allan. Chapter 6.

Cobham, D. *The Economics of International Trade.* Woodhead Faulkner/ Lloyds Bank. Chapters 3–5.

CSO. *United Kingdom Balance of Payments.* HMSO (Annual).

Once you feel confident about your knowledge of this topic try to answer the 10 multiple choice questions which follow.

Multiple choice questions

1 Consider the following measures which might be used to help rectify a deficit on the current account. Which one of these items could be described as expenditure reducing rather than expenditure switching:

   a   devaluation or depreciation of the currency?
   b   import quotas?
   c   exchange control regulations?
   d   increase in Excise duty?

 _answer_

2 If a country was operating a system of fixed exchange rates and it experienced a balance of payments deficit which of the following would be the most likely consequence:

   a   reserves of foreign currency would rise?
   b   net outflows on capital account would increase?
   c   a reduction in the size of the budget deficit?
   d   a fall in interest rates in order to encourage investment?

 _answer_

3 Both the freely floating exchange rate and the gold standard are said to bring about an automatic rectification of a balance of payments deficit. However they differ in that:

   a   with the floating exchange rate there is no change in the level of the country's reserves of foreign currency.
   b   on the gold standard the domestic purchasing power of the pound rises whilst with the floating exchange rate the external purchasing power of the pound falls.
   c   only the gold standard is independent of changes in the interest rate.
   d   with the floating exchange rate the level of unemployment will rise whereas with the gold standard employment will be maintained.

 _answer_

4   The invisible account item General Government Services is a net deficit item for the UK. Of the various components which make up this figure the largest single item is:

a   military expenditure.
b   administration and diplomatic expenses.
c   payments to the EEC.
d   payments to the IMF.

 _answer_

5   If the exchange rate of the pound were to depreciate from £1 = $1.40 to £1 = $1.20 and as a result of this the volume of exports to the USA were to increase by 20% the elasticity of demand for exports would be:

a   1.40.
b   0.71.
c   0.83
d   impossible to determine from these figures.

 _answer_

6   The J-curve effect shows that:

a   any surplus on the balance of payments overall must at some time be followed by corresponding deficits.
b   there tends to be regular fluctuations between deficit and surplus on the balance of payments.
c   following measures to improve the balance of payments, such as devaluation, there tends to be an immediate deterioration in the balance before subsequent recovery.
d   it is necessary for expenditure reducing measures to be taken before expenditure switching methods are used as a means of improving the trade balance.

 _answer_

Question 7–10 are based on the following selection of items from a balance of payments statement.

(i)   Exports (F.O.B.)
(ii)   Sea transport
(iii)   Interest profits and dividends

(iv)   Overseas investment in the UK

(v)   Change in official reserves.

7   Which of these items appear in the current account:

   a   (i) only?
   b   (i) and (ii) only?
   c   (i), (ii) and (iii) only?
   d   (i), (ii), (iii) and (iv) only?

 *answer*

8   Which of these items are always net credits (+) in the UK's account:

   a   (i) only?
   b   (i) and (ii) only?
   c   (i), (iii) and (iv) only?
   d   (ii) and (iii) only?

 *answer*

9   Which of these items appear in the investment and other capital transactions part of the account:

   a   (iii), (iv) and (v) only?
   b   (iv) only?
   c   (iii) and (v) only?
   d   (iv) and (v) only?

 *answer*

10   Which of these items appear in the 'invisibles' section of the account:

   a   (ii) only?
   b   (ii) and (iii) only?
   c   (ii), (iii) and (iv) only?
   d   (ii), (iii), (iv) and (v) only?

 *answer*

 Answers follow on pages 128–132. Score 2 marks for each correct answer.

Answers

1 The correct answer is **d**.

Measures which a government might use to rectify a current account deficit may be divided into:
- *expenditure reducing* — those which clamp down on domestic expenditure
- *expenditure switching* — those which by restricting imports switch expenditure to domestically produced goods

You should have realised that the first three possibilities are of an expenditure switching nature. Devaluation (answer **a**) seeks to increase the demand for exports and decrease the demand for imports. Import quotas (answer **b**) put a restriction on the quantity of imports, thus causing people to switch to domestically produced goods. Exchange control regulations (answer **c**) by preventing people from changing money into foreign currency cause them to spend the money at home.

We have been a little tricky with the correct answer **d** because you may think of excise duty as a tax on imports. But excise is a tax on certain products *wherever* they are produced e.g. excise on beer, petrol etc. So increasing duty is just like increasing any other tax and is therefore an expenditure reducing measure.

2 The correct answer is **c**.

If in answer **c** we had said that the government would run a budget surplus then it would immediately be apparent that it would be an expenditure reducing measure designed to rectify the deficit. However, we have stated it in the more realistic manner of reducing the budget deficit. This will have a deflating effect on the economy. You should remember that with a fixed exchange rate deflation is the most likely method of rectifying deficit.

Answer **a** is patently incorrect since a deficit would *reduce* the reserves of foreign currency. When we come to answer **b** we must consider that the outflow of capital is more likely to be a *cause* of a deficit rather than a *consequence* of it. Indeed most governments would seek to discourage or prevent the outflow of capital when faced with a deficit. Answer **d** is also incorrect since the deficit is likely to lead to an increase in interest rates both to encourage inward investment and to deflate the economy.

3 The correct answer is **b**.

It is still worth studying the gold standard because it is most instructive in explaining the nature of exchange rates and also because it has many parallels with the regime of floating rates. However, there are important differences as is highlighted by the question.

If the country is on the gold standard then a deficit will cause an outflow of money and therefore deflation — in the true sense of the word, that is to say a fall in the price level. Which is another way of saying the *purchasing power of the pound will rise*. However, with a floating exchange rate the value of the pound against other currencies will decline. Giving us the correct answer **b**. Thus both systems work by adjusting prices but with the gold standard it is all prices, both domestic and export, which are affected, whereas with the floating rates it is just the export prices which fall as the pound depreciates.

Answer **a** is incorrect, for although a floating rate may reduce the drain on resources by doing away with the need to support the currency, a deficit is nonetheless likely to lead to a fall in reserves. When we consider answer **c** we find that it is also incorrect since changes in interest rates are used to defend exchange rates irrespective of the regime in operation. In answer **d** the correct order has been reversed. It is under a gold standard that a deficit will cause unemployment which is a good reason for having floating rates.

4   The correct answer is **a**.

You will have to know your balance of payment account well (or have been lucky) to get this one correct. Not that it is difficult to understand, simply that you will have to know the composition of items in the account precisely.

From the options given only two (**a** and **b**) actually come in the General Government Services Account. Of these two, military expenditure overseas is by far the greatest, being well over £1 billion. Of this, the majority goes to support British forces in Germany.

You may be forgiven if you have chosen **c** as the correct answer. EEC payments do feature in the General Government Services sector but these are payments *from* the EEC institution to the UK and are relatively minor. The bulk of the UK's transactions with the EEC are not under this section but under that of Transfers.

You should not have chosen **d** because you should be aware that dealings with the IMF come under the Official Financing part of the account.

5   The correct answer is **a**.

We are concerned here with calculating the coefficient of the elasticity of demand for exports. Which is:

$$E = \frac{\textbf{percentage change in volume of exports}}{\textbf{percentage change in price}}$$

Thus we would have:

$$E = \frac{\Delta X/X}{\Delta P/P}$$

where ΔX = changes in volume of exports
X = original volume of exports
ΔP = change in price $\left.\vphantom{\begin{array}{c}a\\b\end{array}}\right\}$ i.e. exchange rate
P = original price

In our example we would obtain

$$\frac{0.2}{0.2/1.4} \quad \text{(given in the question)}$$

rearranged to give

$$0.2 \times \frac{1.4}{0.2} = 1.4$$

The other answers are obtained by inverting the equation and by using the wrong base (1.2) for the change in the exchange rate.

6 The correct answer is **c**.

Figure 6.2 illustrates a J-curve — its appearance gives rise to its name. As you can see it plots the current account balance (+) or (−) against time. It is thus answer **c** which gives the correct description of this. The effect comes about because of:

(a) Insufficient capacity when the economy is at, or near, capacity. In which case expenditure switching policies are unlikely to be successful immediately until capacity can be increased.

(b) Measures taken to rectify a deficit may cause a crisis of confidence, thereby leading to an outflow of money which leads to a deterioration in the payments position before the (hoped for) recovery.

The existence of the J-curve effect is an argument for taking expenditure-reducing measures to create capacity in the economy preparatory to taking expenditure-switching measures (see answer **d**).

The first answer refers to the fact that there must be an overall balance in the balance of payments. However this is not connected with the J-curve nor is there a regular pattern to deficits and surplus as suggested by answer **b**.

Exam tip: You really should have been able to get answers 7–10 absolutely correct. It is absolutely necessary that you are totally familiar

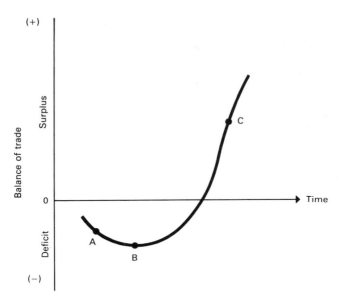

Fig. 6.2

with the main items in the account. Past questions in the examination have even asked students to complete and calculate an account. So you should be sure that you know:

— The chief items in the account.
— Which sections of the account they are placed in.
— Whether they are normally (+) or (−).
— Their meaning and significance.
— Some idea of their relative size.
— You should be able to arrive at a balance (see page 115).

7   The correct answer is **c.**

The current account is the balance of visibles and invisibles. Clearly exports and sea transports are examples of these categories. However, interest profit dividends are also an invisible. Investments appear in the capital account but *income* from them is a current item, much as the inland revenue counts income from your investment as current income.

8   The correct answer is **c.**

There are two types of knowledge necessary to answer this question. First, knowing which items are always (+) in any account e.g. export, and second, those which can be either (+) or (−) but which are always (+) as far as the UK are concerned.

(i) *Exports* must always be a (+) as *imports* must always be a (−).

(ii) *Sea transport* can be either (+) or (−) depending on the circumstances. It always used to be a net gain for the UK but is now frequently a net loss.

(iii) *Interest profits* such as dividends could technically be either (+) or (−) but in fact as far as the UK is concerned are always a substantial (+).

(iv) *Overseas investment* in the UK will always be shown as (+) just as UK investment overseas will be shown as a (−).

(v) *The change in official reserves* can be either (+) or (−) depending upon circumstances. Remember running down the reserves is shown as (+) whereas adding to the reserves is shown as (−). This last point explains why we prefer to use (+) and (−) for expanding items rather than debit or credit.

We are thus left with (i), (iii) and (iv) (answer **c**) as the items which are (+) *for the UK*.

9   The correct answer is **b**.

We have already explained that items (i), (ii) and (iii) are in the current account which leaves us with the last two. Obviously, overseas investment in the UK (iv) falls with the capital transaction section but the change in reserves does *not* it is shown under official financing. Thus answer **b** is correct.

10   The correct answer is **b**.

Exports (i) are obviously visible trade and therefore cannot be correct in this question. As explained in the previous answer items (iv) and (v) fall into other sections of the account. This leaves us with (ii) and (iii) on the invisibles.

Score 2 marks for each correct answer. What was your score? Fill it in on the score grid.

If you scored 12 or less and are still a bit shaky on some points go back and look at the study guide again before proceeding with the post-test.

If you are sure you really understand and are familiar with this topic now, try the 10 further questions which are on pages 205–207. Alternatively you can go on to your next topic and do all the post-tests together at the end.

Topic 7 Exchange rates

Study guide

Exchange rates are a complex topic demanding a thorough knowledge of
the economics of the market place as well as an understanding of the
principles particular to international trade. An additional problem we

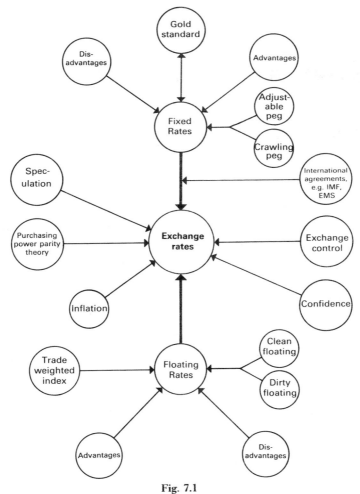

Fig. 7.1

face is the *bias of nationalism*. Many countries have wasted vast sums of money supporting unrealistic rates. Consider the vocabulary which is used if the exchange rate is high; we are said to have 'a strong pound'; conversely, a low rate is described as 'weak' and the papers often speak of 'defending the pound'. These are very emotive words. However, what is important is not that the exchange rate be low or high but that it should be *correct for the circumstances.*

To be confident about the topic, you must be familiar with all the items in Figure 7.1. At the top of the diagram we see the factors concerning fixed exchange rates and at the bottom, those concerning floating rates. The items clustered around the centre, such as confidence, affect all types of exchange rates. When you have finished this topic and also Topics 8 and 9, return to this diagram and make sure that you can explain all the items in it.

The determination of exchange rates

Let us begin with exports and imports as the starting point for our understanding of exchange rates.

Let us suppose that the only reason for changing money is for foreign trade. That is to say, if people from the UK wish to buy foreign goods then they must obtain foreign currency with which to effect their purchase. It is no good, for example, offering a French vintner pounds sterling for wine; he will demand francs. Similarly, if foreigners wish to buy UK goods then UK manufacturers will demand pounds in return for them. The exchange rate will be determined by the demand and supply for exports and imports.

The exchange rate for any particular currency is the result of export demand and import supply.

In Figure 7.2 we have measured all foreign currencies in dollars. Thus, foreigners wishing to buy UK goods offer dollars for them; this, therefore, constitutes the *demand for sterling.* Conversely, UK people offer pounds in order to purchase foreign goods. Thus, the *demand for imports* constitutes the *supply of pounds* to the foreign exchange market.

The exchange rate is now determined like any other price. In Figure 7.2 we can see that the exchange rate is £1 = $1.60 or that $1 costs 62.5 pence. It is, therefore, possible for us to analyse changes in exchange rates in the same manner as other prices.

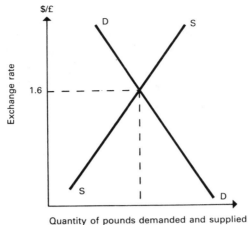

Fig. 7.2

Changes in the exchange rate

Changes in exports and imports can be shown as rightward or leftward shifts in the curves. For example, in Figure 7.3a we see the effect of an increased demand for UK exports; foreigners are therefore offering more money so that demand for sterling increases. Thus, the price of foreign currency has declined and the pound is said to have *appreciated*. If foreign currency becomes more expensive the pound is said to have *depreciated*.

An appreciation in the rate of exchange could therefore be caused by either:

* an increased demand for UK exports; or
* a decreased UK demand for imports.

Alternatively, a depreciation in the rate of exchange could be caused by:

* an increased UK demand for imports;
* a reduced foreign demand for UK exports.

In Figure 7.3a we see that the shift to the right in the demand curve for pounds in the foreign exchange market has caused the pound to appreciate from £1 = $1 to £1 = $1.50. Alternatively, the price of $1 has fallen from £1 to £0.66.

What does the diagram in Figure 7.3b show? Well, in fact it shows exactly the same thing. That is to say that if we can show the demand and supply for pounds in dollars we can also show the demand and supply for dollars in pounds. If there is an increase in the demand for British exports this can be shown as an increase in the supply of dollars

(a)

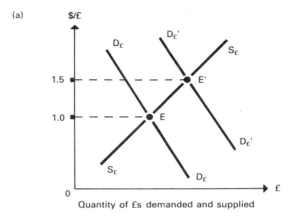

Quantity of £s demanded and supplied

(b)

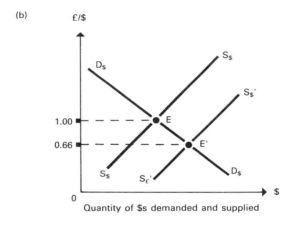

Quantity of $s demanded and supplied

Fig. 7.3

being offered for UK exports. In Figure 7.3b we see that this causes the price of $1 to fall from £1 to $0.66.

Other factors influencing exchange rates

1   **Non-trade influences.** So far we have discussed exchange rates as being determined by the demand for imports and exports. However, exchange rates are influenced by many other factors such as invisible trade, interest rates, capital movements, speculation and government activities.

2   Confidence is a vital factor in determining exchange rates. This is especially so because large companies 'buy forward' i.e. they purchase foreign currency ahead of their needs. They are, therefore, very sensitive to factors which may influence future rates. Key indicators are such things as inflation and government policy. So the exchange rate at any particular moment is more likely to reflect the anticipated situation in a country rather than the present one.

3   Inflation. Let us assume the UK has inflation but the USA does not. This will mean that the sterling price of UK goods will rise. Other things being equal, the demand for UK goods will therefore decrease, while American goods will now appear cheaper to Britons who will consequently buy more. Thus, the demand for sterling will decrease while the demand for dollars will increase and both the factors will cause a depreciation in the external value of sterling. If, on the other hand, the domestic rate of inflation is lower than that abroad, these factors may be expected to work in reverse.

 Consider diagrams (a) and (b) in Figure 7.3. How would you show the effect of an increased UK demand for American exports?

The situation we have described has had no government intervention and can be termed a *freely floating exchange rate* or a *clean float*.

Fixed exchange rates

The alternative to a freely floating exchange rate is that the government fixes the exchange rate. The earliest methods of doing this were through the gold standard. Although the idea of the gold standard may seem a little out of date now, we can learn a great deal about fixed exchange rates by studying it.

The gold standard

A gold standard occurs when a unit of a country's currency is valued in terms of a specific amount of gold. The Gold Standard Act of 1870 fixed the value of the pound sterling such that 1 ounce of gold cost £3.17s.10½d. This remained constant until 1914.

There are several types of gold standard. A **full gold standard** is where gold coins circulate freely in the economy and paper money is *fully convertible* into gold. Such was the case in the UK until 1914. A **gold bullion standard** is when gold is available in bullion form (bars) for foreign trade only. The UK adopted such a standard in 1925 which lasted until 1931. A **gold exchange standard** occurs when a country fixes the value of its currency, not in gold, but in terms of other currency which is on the gold standard. For example, from 1925–31 most Commonwealth and Empire countries fixed their exchange rates by quoting their currency against sterling.

After the 1939–45 war the USA maintained the price of gold at $35 for 1 ounce. However, in 1971 the USA was forced to abandon this and it is unlikely that a gold standard of any type will be readopted in the near future.

The gold standard and the balance of payments

One of the most notable features of the gold standard is that a country operating it will experience automatic rectification of any balance of payments disequilibrium.

Consider what would happen if a country had a payments deficit. In order to pay for the deficit, gold would be exported for gold was, and is, almost universally accepted. However, this would reduce the money supply in the country because the money supply is tied to gold. The result of this would be deflation. The country's exports would become cheaper and its imports dearer. Other things being equal, this should bring the country's payments back into equilibrium. The effect of a surplus would be eliminated by this process working in reverse through inflation.

Floating exchange rates also automatically regulate the balance of payments. However, there is an important difference from the gold standard. With the gold standard an imbalance is rectified by changes in the *internal* level of economic activity; deflation, for example, would bring about unemployment which would reduce the consumption of imports. With floating exchange rates the balance is brought about by a change in the *external* value of the currency. That is to say, depreciation of the exchange rate reduces the price of exports (but not the domestic price) while increasing the price of imports.

Pegged exchange rates

When a country is not on a gold standard but wishes to have a fixed exchange rate, this can be done by the government 'pegging' the exchange rate i.e. a rate is fixed and then guaranteed by the government. For example, after the UK left the gold standard in 1931 the government fixed the price of sterling against the dollar and made the rate of £1 = $4.03 effective by agreeing to buy or sell any amount of currency at this price.

Exchange control

One of the methods by which a government can attempt to make the stated exchange rate effective is through exchange control. Exchange control refers to restrictions placed upon the ability of citizens to exchange foreign currency freely. For example in 1966 the UK government would only allow Britons to convert £50 into foreign currency for holidays abroad. The Mitterand government in France imposed similar restrictions in 1983. The Conservative government abolished all forms of exchange control in 1979. Britons, however, may still find themselves subject to restrictions by other countries, for example, anyone travelling in Eastern Europe becomes acutely aware of strict exchange controls.

The adjustable peg

This was a system of fixed exchange rates operated by the members of the International Monetary Fund from 1947 to 1971. Members agreed not to let the value of their currencies vary by more than 1% either side of a parity. For example, the UK's exchange rate in 1949 was £1 = $2.80 and sterling was allowed to appreciate to £1 = $2.82 or depreciate to £1 = $2.78. The system was termed 'adjustable' because it was possible for a country to devalue or revalue in the event of serious disequilibrium. Some countries operated a so-called 'crawling peg'. Under this system a currency was allowed to depreciate (or appreciate) by a small percentage each year. If, for example, a limit of 2% was set and the currency devalued by this amount in year 1, it would be allowed to devalue by another 2% in year 2, and so on.

For and against fixed exchange rates

The chief advantage of fixed exchange rates is that they give certainty to international trade and investors. It is also said that they reduce speculation. Fixed exchange rates also impose discipline on domestic economic policies because, in the event of an adverse balance of payments deflationary measures will have to be taken to restore the situation.

On the other hand, if an exchange rate is fixed incorrectly, this will cause intense speculation against the currency. It can often be an expensive job defending a fixed exchange rate, requiring large reserves of foreign exchange. Defending a currency may also involve raising interest rates and this can be both costly and damaging to the domestic economy. It is possible, therefore, that a fixed exchange rate may result in domestic policy being subordinated to the external situation.

Despite a great desire by many politicians to return to fixed exchange rates, it is extremely unlikely that it will be possible while rates of inflation between countries continue to differ so greatly.

If we speak of floating rates rather than fixed rates then the arguments are reversed. You will see the main points summarized in Figure 7.4.

Fixed rates	
Advantages	*Disadvantages*
1 Greater certainty to international trade 2 Less speculation — but speculation still possible if rate overvalued or undervalued 3 Discipline on internal dealings	1 Greater need for official reserves 2 Possibility of setting rate wrongly 3 Inflation makes maintenance of fixed rates difficult 4 Internal policy subordinated to need to maintain exchange rate
Floating rates	
1 Automatic stabilization of balance of payments disequilitoria 2 Frees internal policy from external constraints 3 Flexibility 4 Lower need for reserves 5 Absence of crisis 6 Possibility of management and manipulation 7 Insulates domestic economy from inflation elsewhere	1 Greater uncertainty 2 Lack of investment caused by greater uncertainty 3 More speculation 4 Lack of discipline in internal economy

Fig. 7.4 *The exchange rate debate*

Theories of exchange rates

We have considered some of the factors which can influence exchange rates. However, there is no completely satisfactory theory that explains how the equilibrium rate of exchange is established. In Figure 7.2 we might make the assumption that the equilibrium rate will occur at the intersection of the curves when the balance of payments is in equilibrium and that imbalances will cause shifts to new equilibriums.

However, we still would like to explain why the exchange rate occurs at the level it does, e.g. why is it £1 = \$2 and not £1 = \$3 and so on. The Swedish economist Gustav Cassell, building on the idea of the classical economist and mercantalists, attempted to explain this in terms of purchasing power parity.

1 *The purchasing power parity theory* suggests, for example, that the exchange rate would be in equilibrium if a situation existed where the same 'basket of goods' which costs £100 in the UK cost DM380 in West Germany and the exchange rate were £1 = DM3.80. In order to do this, we would have to discount transport costs and tariffs. A measure we might use could appear as:

$$\text{Purchasing power parity} = \frac{\textbf{West German consumer price index}}{\textbf{UK consumer price index}}$$

From this we might deduce that a doubling of the general price level in the UK while prices in West Germany remained constant would lead to the exchange rate being cut by one half. However, no such strict proportionality exists. There are a number of reasons for this.

(a) The 'basket of goods' which determines domestic price levels is different from the goods which are traded internationally. Items which are important domestically, such as housing, bread, rail fares, etc. do not influence foreign trade significantly.

(b) Exchange rates are influenced by many other factors such as capital movements, speculation and interest rates.

(c) Confidence is also a very significant factor in determining exchange rates.

We may conclude that although domestic price levels do influence exchange rates, there is no strict proportionality.

2 *The portfolio balance theory.* While the purchasing power parity theory concentrates on the trade in imports and exports, the theory of portfolio balance stresses the importance of international investment flows, including speculative flows, in determining exchange rates. It assumes that large investors are aware of investment opportunities worldwide. They therefore diversify their portfolios to gain higher yield and to reduce risk. This makes investment sensitive to relative yields in different countries. For example, if the yield on, say, Treasury bills in London were to increase then you would expect funds to flow in from other countries. This in turn would exert an upward pressure on the sterling exchange rate.

The huge amount of highly liquid funds in international markets makes interest rates a key factor in determining exchange rates. However, *expectations* of future interest rates and/or exchange rates may be *more* important than the existing rates. This leads us to the interest rate parity theory.

3 *The interest rate parity theory.* In the era of floating exchange rates much currency is brought 'forward'. For example, a company which may need large quantities of deutschemarks in 6 months time may place an order for them now and both buyer and seller agree to exchange the currency in 6 months's time at the rate stated today. This rate may be higher or lower than today's rate depending upon *expectations* of the future. Needless to say, there is also a very great speculative market in currency futures.

If the UK total bill for exports and imports and all other invisible items for 1986 was approximately $200b, this would give an average day's requirement of approximately $56m. Speculative movements greatly increase this.

Out of interest, what do you think is a likely amount for a good days' dealing on the London foreign exchange market?

Check your answer on page 145.

Now can you understand the crucial importance of:
— expectations
— confidence
— interest rates
— speculation
in determining exchange rates?

The interest rate parity theory suggests that differences in interest rates between countries will be reflected in the discount or premium at which currency futures are traded.

The picture is complicated by the difference between 'real' and 'nominal' interest rates, i.e. the rate of inflation and expectations of future rates of inflation.

Forward rates

Figure 7.5 shows the sterling 'spot' and 'forward' rates for selective countries. Where a currency is traded at a premium there is an expectation that the rate will rise and that the rate will fall where currency is traded at a discount.

	Closing Market Rates	One Month Forward Rates	
Canada	2·0288 −2·0338	0·51c. to 0·41c.	premium
Germany	3·5616 −3·5697	2·50 to 2·25 pfgs	premium
Sweden	11·02 − 11·05	0·125 to 0·75 ore	discount
Switzerland	3·02 −3·03	2·375c. to 2·125c.	premium
USA	1·4555 − 1·4570	0·5c. to 0·54c.	premium

Fig. 7.5

Why are there two figures in the closing market rates? Well, if you don't know look at the exchange rates board in your own bank. Note how much closer these market rates are than tourist rates.

Recent experience of exchange rates

We discuss the operation of the International Monetary Fund in detail in Topic 8, so here we are going to consider how developments since the early 1970s have influenced the UK economy.

Dirty floating

Following the USA's abandonment of the gold standard in 1971 and the failure of the Smithsonian agreement, the UK floated the pound in 1972. The objective of the government was that the development of the economy should be free to continue without the constraint of having to maintain a fixed exchange rate. Although ostensibly the government allowed the exchange rate to find its own level, it in fact interfered and manipulated the exchange rate. This is termed **managed flexibility**, or, more memorably, a 'dirty float'.

Figure 7.6 illustrates government intervention in the foreign exchange market. Left to itself the exchange rate would be $£1 = \$1$ but the government forces the rate up to $£1 = \$1.90$ by buying sterling on the

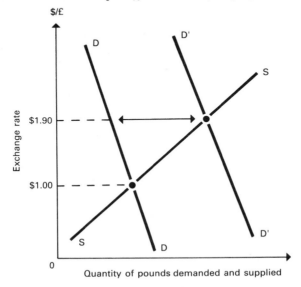

Fig. 7.6

foreign exchange market, thereby shifting the demand curve to the right.

Since the oil crisis of 1973 most countries have used floating exchange rates. There are some regional attempts to fix rates such as the EMS.

The government agency responsible for intervention in the foreign exchange market is the Exchange Equalisation Account. This was set up in 1932 following the UK's abandonment of the gold standard. It is controlled by the Treasury and managed by the Bank of England. Its object is to buy and sell sterling for gold or foreign exchange in order to stabilize the exchange rate. In times of fixed exchange rates the Account has sometimes lost large sums of money defending an unrealistic rate. Since the float of 1972 the operation of the account has been more muted but it is its actions which give rise to the term 'dirty float'. Nearly all governments operate a similar system. The Account's operations should not be confused with the 'official financing' of the balance of payments.

Measurement difficulties

When countries are on a gold standard there is a simple way to show the value of their currencies. However, with floating exchange rates it becomes difficult. The most widely known measure of the UK exchange rate is that against the dollar but the dollar itself is floating. It is possible, therefore, for the pound to be rising against the value of the dollar while falling against other currencies such as the yen. *Trade weighted indices* are an attempt to overcome this problem by providing a measure of a currency in terms of a number of currencies which are weighted in accordance with their importance in trade to the country whose currency is being measured. The Bank of England trade weighted index is known as the *sterling effective exchange rate*, based on 1975.

The UK: floating or sinking?

How well has the floating rate worked for the UK? After the UK floated sterling in 1972 the exchange rate was £1 = $1.55. In October 1976 there was an effective devaluation of 40.4%. This massive drop was not altogether unwelcome to the UK government who believed it would make exports more competitive. It should be remembered, however, that increasing the price of imports will also increase inflation. It is reckoned that a 4% rise in import prices causes 1% domestic inflation. The UK government, however, seemed happy to settle for a rate of about £1 = $1.70. But no sooner had the rate stabilized around this level than the prospects of North Sea oil brought money flooding into London and the exchange rate soared, much to the displeasure of the government. It appeared that a pound that floated upward was almost as difficult to live with as a sinking one.

The end of the 1970s saw the UK with a large balance of payments surplus and an exchange rate almost back to the 1971 level. The 'overvalued' pound had UK industry screaming for relief. The pound then collapsed, despite a sound balance of payments, and in 1983 dropped below £1 = $1.50 for the first time. The collapse continued until in early 1985 the rate hovered around £1 = $1.10. However, by the end of the year the rate had recovered to £1 = $1.45. Over the same period the trade weighted index rose from 73.0 to 78.0. The necessity of defending the exchange rate caused interest rates to be held at very high real levels.

We may conclude our discussion of floating exchange rates by saying that there have undoubtedly been unprecedented fluctuations in value but there have also been unprecedented circumstances and it is doubtful if fixed exchange rates could have coped with the situation. Now, however, people are once again beginning to look towards a more stable regime of exchange rates.

Answer to the task on page 142: $49,000,000,000, i.e. $49b. You underestimated a little?

Further reading

Pratt, M.J. *A Guide to the International System.* Banking Information Service. Chapters 1 and 3.

Cobham, H. *The Economics of International Trade.* Woodhead Faulkner/ Lloyds Bank. Chapter 8.

Crockett, A. *Money: Theory Policy and Institutions* 2nd edn. Van Nostrand Reinhold (UK). Chapter 14.

Griffiths and Wall. *Applied Economics.* Longman. Chapter 25.

Beardshaw, J. *Economics: A Student's Guide.* Pitman.

Stanlake, G.F. *Introductory Economics.* Longman.

These last two are to be used if you have difficulty with the economics of demand and supply etc.

Once you feel confident of your knowledge of this topic try to answer the 10 multiple choice questions which follow.

Multiple choice questions

1 The chief advantage of fixed exchange rates is that:

   a a nation can determine the external value of its currency to its own best advantage.

   b it brings stability to a country's external trade.

   c it frees a country's domestic policy from external restraints.

   d there is a reduced need for reserves of foreign currency.

 _answer_

2 Which of the following is *not* a problem with freely fluctuating exchange rates:

   a fundamental disequilibrium in balances of payment continue?

   b future costs of imports are unknown?

   c past debt will be repaid in the future by foreign exchange of unknown cost?

   d speculators may cause unnecessary fluctuations in the exchange rate?

 _answer_

3 When the monetary authorities interfere covertly to influence the determination of a fluctuating rate this is known as:

   a monetary intervention.

   b exchange equalization funding.

   c destabilization.

   d a dirty float.

 _answer_

4 Which of the following is an example of exchange control:

   a government intervention in foreign exchange markets by purchasing foreign currencies?

   b maintenance of a fixed exchange rate?

   c a premium imposed on foreign currencies purchased for the purpose of overseas investment?

d the Bretton Woods Agreement?

 *answer*

5 The purchasing power parity theory suggests:

a freely floating exchange rates will always move towards equilibrium.

b the exchange rate between two currencies depends upon their relative domestic purchasing power.

c exchange rates are determined by the balance of payments situation.

d a nation's purchasing power is determined by relative movements in exchange rates.

 *answer*

6 The interest rate parity theory of foreign exchange rates predict that:

a interest rates are likely to be the same in international markets.

b the rate of return on inward investment is a function of forces in international markets

c the difference in the rates of interest between two countries will be reflected in the rate of discount or premium at which one currency is bought or sold in 'forward' markets against each other.

d exchange rates are determined by the international movement of capital and of 'hot' money.

 *answer*

Questions 7 to 9 are based on Figure 7.7 which shows the quantity of pounds sterling demanded and supplied on the foreign exchange market. The initial supply and demand curves are shown by the unbroken lines. The broken lines show the situations which might occur after various changes have taken place.

In each question, starting from the original equilibrium exchange rate of X, and presuming that *only* the changes stated occur, determine whether the new equilibrium lies on curve **a b c** or **d**.

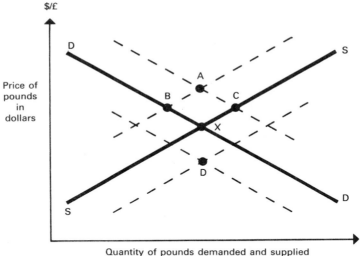

Fig. 7.7

7　American owned firms in the UK reduce their dividend payments below the previous level.

8　American tourists spend more money in the UK.

9　The UK purchases Trident missiles from the USA and there is a fall in demand for UK exports.

10　This question is based on Figure 7.8 which shows the exchange rate of the £ against the deutschemark and the quantity of pounds sterling supplied. The slope of this particular supply curve is the result of the fact that the:

a　demand for imports is elastic.
b　demand for imports is inelastic.
c　supply of DM's is limited.
d　government has interfered with the exchange rate.

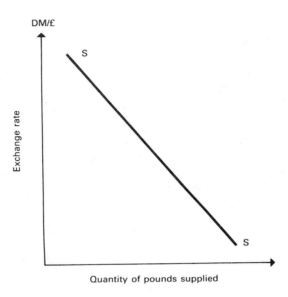

Fig. 7.8

Answers follow on pages 150–155. Score 2 marks for each correct answer.

Answers

1   The correct answer is **b**.

This is a straightforward question concerned with the advantages (and disadvantages) of a fixed exchange rate. It is argued that the greatest advantage of a fixed exchange rate is the stability it brings to trade. Exporters and importers are certain of the cost of orders and this therefore encourages trade. (For example no more holiday surcharges!)

Answer **a** may seem tempting but if a country *overvalues* its currency it will be faced with the cost of supporting it or of imposing strict exchange control. If currency is undervalued then domestic consumers will suffer because imports will be artificially expensive.

The remaining answers are advantages of a *floating rate* not a fixed rate. With a fixed rate the government must rectify any imbalance by deflating (or inflating) the domestic economy so answer **c** is wrong. It is usually the case that a country will require *bigger* reserves to support a fixed rate, answer **d** is therefore also wrong.

2   The correct answer is **a**.

This question is also asking you about the advantages and disadvantages of different types of exchange rate. The wording of the correct answer (**a**) is a little difficult but it should be obvious that the remaining answers *are* problems associated with floating rates. With answers **b** and **c** we are concerned with the uncertainty factor which floating rates introduce. This will obviously affect both the price of imports (answer **b**) and the cost of servicing a foreign debt (answer **c**) since foreign debts must be paid in foreign currency.

We would normally say that one of the chief advantages of a floating exchange rate is that it automatically rectifies any balance of payments disequilibrium by either appreciating or depreciating the external prices of the currency. Thus, the continuance of disequilibrium (answer **a**) is *not* a problem, therefore, is the correct answer.

3   The correct answer is **d**.

If, with a floating exchange rate, the authorities leave the rate to be entirely determined by market forces, it is termed a 'clean float'. More usually the government would interfere to influence the exchange rate, and this practice is correctly termed *managed flexibility*. It is often the case that the authorities do this covertly (secretly) in which case it is termed a dirty float (see study guide).

As far as the other answers are concerned answer **a** is not a recognized expression to describe any process either domestically or externally, although you could argue that the government is interfering monetarily! Answer **c** is plainly wrong since the object of intervention is to stabilize not to destabilize. You can be forgiven if you chose answer **b** since you clearly knew that stabilization is usually carried out by the Exchange Equalisation Account. However, this is not a funding operation. (Remember funding is correcting a short-term debt to a longer-term one, see Topic 5.)

4 The correct answer is **c**.

Exchange control is placing restrictions on the ability of people to change one currency into another. Of the available answers only **c** fits the bill. In fact Britain operated such a policy up to 1979. If a Briton wished to purchase dollars for investment purposes the Bank of England imposed a surcharge of 25% which was known as the **dollar premium**. This was repayable when the investment was sold. In the UK all exchange control regulations were abolished in 1979.

Government nearly always interferes in foreign exchange markets (answer **a**) whether on fixed or floating rates and whether or not there is exchange control. Thus **b** is also wrong, although some type of exchange control is often associated with fixed exchange rates.

The Bretton Woods Agreement set up the IMF and its objective was to do away with restrictions rather than increase them. We hope you didn't choose answer **d**!

5 The correct answer is **b**.

Answer **b** is a fairly succinct statement of the theory. Check in the study guide if you are not sure on this point.

Answer **a** is true but is nothing to do with the purchasing power parity theory. Under a regime of freely floating rates it may be the case that exchange rates are largely determined by the balance of payments situation, (answer **c**) but again this is not purchasing power parity. Finally, it is only the *external* purchasing power of currency which is determined by exchange rates and therefore answer **d** is also incorrect.

6 The correct answer is **c**.

The interest rate parity theory is much less well known than the purchasing power parity theory, though much more demonstrable. It suggests that if there are differences in real rates of interest between two markets having taken account of other factors e.g. risk, then this will lead to currency being sold either at a discount (lower rate) or premium (higher rate). When people agree to buy or sell currency in the future (the forward market), the discount or premium will reflect the anticipation that rates of interest will tend to equalize in the future.

It may appear from the above that answer a ought to be correct. But clearly interest rates are different. The interest rate parity theory draws our attention to the importance of *expectations* of the future in the determination of interest rates and exchange rates.

The rate of return on investment is determined by many factors but it is nothing to do with the interest rate parity theory and therefore answer b is also wrong. Exchange rates may be greatly influenced by the movements of capital and 'hot' money but they are also determined by the current account of the balance of payments, by the relative rates of inflation etc. Thus, answer d is wrong on any estimation.

Questions 7–9. When considering the graphical analysis of exchange rates it is always necessary to pay careful attention to the labelling of the axes. In this case we are looking at the supply and demand of *pounds* in foreign exchange markets. Thus, on the vertical axis we have the *dollar price of pounds*. This presentation always seems more intelligible to us because we are used to viewing the exchange rate as the *dollar price* and an appreciation of the pound moves us up the price axis. However, you could argue equally logically for putting the demand and supply for *dollars* on the horizontal axis and the *pound price of dollars* on the vertical axis. In this presentation everything becomes reversed; what was the supply of pounds now becomes the demand for dollars etc. and an appreciation of the pound moves us *down* the price axis i.e. the price of a dollar to a Briton has fallen.

Now check your answers to questions 7–9 carefully. Remember all the time that nothing else changes except the condition which is stated in the question.

If you still do not see where you went wrong go back to the study guide where the points above are explained and illustrated. If you are having difficulty you must certainly do this before grappling with question 10.

7 The correct answer is **b**.

The American firm in the UK would obviously pay its dividends in pounds. These pounds would then be exported to the USA in exchange for dollars to pay the American shareholders. By reducing dividends the company has reduced the supply of pounds in the foreign exchange market; the supply curve moves to the left and moves us to point **b**.

Now move back to point X before considering the solution to question 8.

8 The correct answer is **c**.

This the most straightforward of the three questions and so you should have got it right! Increased tourism in the UK means that there is an increase in the demand for pounds; the demand curve moves to the right and moves us to point **c**.

Puzzled? Why is it not an increased supply of dollars?

Because the diagram does not show the demand or the supply of *dollars* — but of *pounds*. So, an increased supply of dollars is shown as an increased demand for pounds.

Return to point X before considering the solution to question 9.

9 The correct answer is **d**.

Since we are considering *two* changes only two answers are possible **a** or **d**. A commonsense response should tell us that both the factors would cause the value of the pound to fall. Therefore the answer must be **d**.

Here is an example of this. The purchase of Trident missiles will increase the supply of pounds shifting the supply curve to the right. Then the fall in demand for exports decreases the demand for pounds moving us to point **d**.

10 The correct answer is **b**.

This is a very tricky question, especially if you do not have a background in economics. And so if you got it right *and* you understand why you are clearly going to do well with this topic.

We will deal with this by taking an example. Consider the situation of a West German wine producer who sells wine in West Germany at DM8 per bottle. The same wine is sold in the UK at £2 per bottle when the exchange rate is £1 = DM4. However, if the exchange rate were to change to £1 = DM2 then, in order to recover the same DM2 per bottle, the UK price must now increase to £4 per bottle.

The effect of this price change upon the supply of sterling to the foreign exchange market is determined by the elasticity of demand for wine in the UK. If demand is elastic then people reduce wine consumption substantially and the supply of sterling falls. This is shown in Figure 7.9a. If demand is unitary then the amount of sterling offered remains constant and thus the supply curve is vertical. This is shown in Figure 7.9b. However, if demand is inelastic then, despite the price rise, people go on drinking and, therefore, in response to a price rise the supply of pound *increases* and we have a perverse supply curve. In Figure 7.9c you can see that, as the exchange rate has fallen from £1 = DM4 to £1 = DM2, that is the price of wine in the UK has increased, the

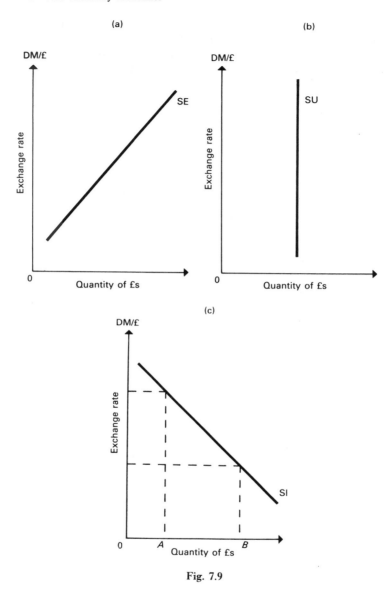

Fig. 7.9

supply of sterling has expanded from OA to OB. Such a condition is likely to cause instability in foreign exchange markets.

If you are still at sea on these last two questions it is almost certainly because your command of basic economics is weak. This being the case you should turn to a basic economics textbook. Read up on demand and supply and elasticity. I have recommended some in the *further reading* on this unit. You will also find more information on other topics, such as the balance of payments, in these textbooks.

Score 2 marks for each correct answer. What was your score? Fill it in on the score grid.

If you scored 12 points or less and are still a bit shaky on some points go back and look at the study guide again before proceeding any further.

If you are sure you really understand and are familiar with this topic now, try the 10 further questions which are on pages 208–210. Alternatively you can go on to your next topic and do all the post-tests together at the end.

Topic 8   International liquidity

Study guide

The last two topics in this study guide are largely descriptive. That is to say, you simply *must know the facts* — the conceptual elements are not so great as in, say, monetary theory. So we must once again stress the importance of keeping up to date.
— Read newspapers and keep clippings
— Make notes from the textbooks
— Keep up-to-date from the radio and TV
You will find that this topic is largely concerned with international institutions. In the past, questions have varied from the obvious on the IMF to the more exotic such as the Asian Development Bank. Thus, if you intend to make this one of your areas of study you must make sure that you have a *wide* knowledge of the topic.

International liquidity

One of the major problems facing the financial world is that of international liquidity — or rather lack of it! We may define official international liquidity as:
Those official reserves which can be used for settling payments imbalances.
Up to the 1930s gold fulfilled this role. Since 1945 international liquidity has consisted mainly of international reserve currencies such as the dollar and of gold.

In this topic we shall examine the institutional arrangements which have been used to try and overcome the problems of the lack of a universally accepted means of international payment.

It will become clear to you that we are talking of the official reserves held by central banks and other monetary authorities. These are a relatively small amount when compared with the vast amount of money (unofficial liquidity) traded in currency markets such as the eurocurrency market. Indeed, the imbalance between official reserves and the amount of currency traded worldwide is one of the problems of international liquidity. Stabilizing exchange rates is very difficult for the authorities because of the lack of reserves.

 Suggest two reasons why stabilizing exchange rates has become more difficult since 1973.

The major institution which has been concerned with international liquidity is the International Monetary Fund (IMF) and despite the collapse of its system of exchange rates in the 1970s it remains important both as a provider of liquidity and as a forum for international debate and co-operation.

The international monetary fund

The Bretton Woods Conference

The IMF is the result of this conference which took place at Bretton Woods (USA). The aim was to try to achieve freer convertibility, improve liquidity and avoid the economic nationalism which had characterized the inter-war years. Britain's representative was Keynes. He had a plan for an international unit of currency. This he called **bancor**. It was to be a hypothetical unit of account against which all other currencies would be measured. This would be administered by a world bank with which all countries would have an account. In effect this bank would perform the task of an ordinary bank, except its customers would be nations: cheques would be written out to settle international indebtedness; money would be created to finance trade; and overdrafts could be given to those countries which required them. It was essential to the concept of the bank, however, that it be allowed to determine each country's exchange rate and adjust it to ensure that nations did not fall hopelessly into debt or run gigantic surpluses. The plan foundered because nations, none more so than the UK, were unwilling to allow an international institution to determine the value of their currency. (Keynes' plan sounded fanciful in 1944 but today SDRs and ECUs, which are international units of account, function well.)

The result was that two compromise institutions were established: in 1947 the International Monetary Fund (IMF); and in 1946 the International Bank for Reconstruction and Development (IBRD). The latter is usually called the World Bank, which is misleading, for it is the IMF which contains the remains of Keynes' idea for the bancor, not the IBRD.

Forty years after its founding the fund had 146 members. This included almost all the countries in the world apart from Switzerland and the Comecon countries (although Rumania and Hungary are members).

Quotas

Each of the members of the IMF is required to contribute a quota to the fund. The size of the quotas will depend upon the national income of the country concerned and upon its share in world trade. The quota used to be made up of 75% in the country's own currency and 25% in gold. Since the demonetization of gold the 25% is now subscribed in reserve assets or SDRs. In this way it was hoped that there would be enough of any currency in the pool for any member to draw on should they get into balance of payments difficulties. Members' quotas are now supplemented by an allocation of SDRs. At 21%, the USA subscribes the largest share of the total allocation of quotas while the UK has the second largest (7.3%).

Voting in the fund is related to the size of the quota. Thus, the advanced industrial countries dominate the fund. The growth of trade and inflation has meant that the quotas have had to be revised upwards on seven occasions.

Borrowing

Originally each member of the Fund could borrow in *tranches* (slices) equivalent to 25% of their quota, taking up to five consecutive tranches, i.e. it was possible to borrow the equivalent of 125% of one's quota. Today it is possible to borrow up to the equivalent of 450% of one's quota over a 3 year period. This is not, however, an unconditional right to borrow. The fund may, and usually does, impose conditions of increasing severity upon a member as it increases its borrowing.

One of the fundamental problems remains the lack of liquidity. Naturally governments resist the pressure to increase their quotas. Instead many schemes have been devised to augment the basic quota arrangements. Some of the most important are:

(a) **Standby arrangements** which work rather like an overdraft facility.

(b) **GAB (General Agreement to Borrow)**. The 10 richest nations got together in 1961 to help each other out in the event of payments imbalances. They now offer aid to less developed countries. GAB has funds of SDR17 billion available.

(c) **Compensatory finance scheme**, now responsible for about one third of all Fund lending.

(d) **Buffer stock facility** to help primary producers finance buffer stocks, e.g. tin.

(e) **Extended fund facility**. Longer-term assistance to members in fundamental payments difficulties.

(f) **Supplementary financing facility** to give longer-term loans to less developed countries.

Special drawing rights (SDRs)

In 1967 it was decided to create international liquidity for the first time. This was done by giving members an allocation of *special drawing rights*. These do not exist as notes but merely as bookkeeping entries. When they were introduced in 1970 they were linked to the dollar and thus to gold (SDR1 = $1) and became known as 'paper gold'. However, since 1974 the value of a unit of SDR has been calculated by combining the value of leading currencies. Originally based on 16 currencies in 1981, this was reduced to 5. The weights used in 1985 are shown in Table 8.1. SDRs are the nearest equivalent to Keynes's idea of bancor so far.

Table 8.1   Percentage weights in SDR currency 'basket'

Currency	%
US dollar	42
Deutschemark	19
Japanese yen	13
French franc	13
Pound sterling	13

The adjustable peg

At the heart of the IMF system was the regime of fixed exchange rates known as the adjustable peg (see page 139). When the UK joined the Fund in 1947 her exchange rate was £1 = $4.03. In 1949 the UK, along with most other countries, devalued against the dollar so that the rate became £1 = $2.80. This rate lasted until 1967 when Britain devalued to £1 = $2.40. The Smithsonian agreement of 1971 was an attempt to patch-up the adjustable peg system and saw the pound revalued to £1 = $2.60.

We will now go on to examine the breakdown of the IMF system — however the IMF itself continues to survive.

The USA leaves the gold standard (1971)

The announcement by President Nixon in August 1971 that the USA would no longer exchange dollars for gold at the official price ended the gold standard. This was forced upon the USA by a massive balance of payments deficit. The fundamental reason for this was realignment of the economic power in the world which had led to massive and continuing surpluses and the accumulation of vast reserves by West Germany and Japan. However, the situation was made worse for the

USA by more immediate circumstances such as the Vietnam war and inflation.

The Smithsonian agreement 1971

The abandonment of the gold standard swept away the adjustable peg system since the world reference point for currencies had disappeared. The Smithsonian agreement of December 1971 was an attempt to re-establish the adjustable peg. This agreement put the value of gold at $38 per ounce, an effective devaluation of the dollar of 8.9%. The agreement has taken its name from the Smithsonian Institute in Washington where it was signed.

The Smithsonian agreement was short-lived, as most countries were obliged to float their currencies in 1972 and 1973. However, two legacies remain. As it was the last time when most currencies were fixed against each other, it is a reference point and one still finds many references to the Smithsonian parities. The other legacy is the European currency snake. Although abandoned in the mid-1970s, it became the EMS in 1979. We describe this later.

The first oil crisis

The instability which was started in 1971 was made much worse by the oil crisis. As a result of the Yom Kippur war of 1973, oil supplies were cut off. When they were resumed the OPEC countries contrived a fourfold rise in price. It is possible to argue that the resulting transfer of money from the developed countries to OPEC nations has brought about one of the most fundamental shifts in economic power of all time. It is estimated that this cost the oil importing countries an extra $100 billion per year. The era of floating the exchange rate combined with the huge dollar surpluses of the OPEC nations were major factors in the rise of the eurocurrency market.

The second oil crisis

In 1978 oil prices were again raised dramatically, this time doubling, and causing a liquidity problem even greater than that of 1973. This price rise was a major factor in the subsequent world depression. This hit the industrialized countries hard but was disastrous for non-oil exporting developing countries (NOEDCs). The subsequent slump in oil prices left some less developed oil exporters such as Mexico saddled with large debts which they found it difficult to service.

The IMF today

In this section we examine how the orderly arrangements of the IMF broke down in the turbulent times of the 1970s. However, the IMF remains an important institution both as a symbol of international cooperation and as a source of liquidity to nations in payment difficulties. At the end of the 1970s many of the major debtor nations such as Mexico, Brazil and Argentina were only bailed out of insolvency by the efforts of the IMF. In addition to this, the IMF is an important lifeline for the very poor nations such as India and Bangladesh. However, the continued existence of the IMF depends upon the support of the major industrialized nations, principally the USA. This was highlighted in September 1983 when the IMF had to suspend all negotiations for loans because of lack of funds.

Between now and the exam, check the financial pages every day and photocopy, or cut out, articles on international liquidity. For example:
— On the debt of third world countries
— Meetings of the IMF

The World Bank

The International Bank for Reconstruction and Development, or World Bank, was set up in 1947 as the sister organization to the IMF. Its original aim was to make loans to develop the war-shattered economies of Europe. The IMF's purpose is not to give loans to finance development projects; this is the job of the IBRD. One of the chief problems facing the IBRD is its lack of funds. Funds come from three sources.

(a) **Quotas.** The membership of the IBRD is the same as that of the IMF. Members make contributions in relation to their IMF quota. Of the quota, 10% is subscribed while the other 90% is promised as a guarantee for the Bank's loans.

(b) **Bonds.** The World Bank sells bonds on the capital markets of the world.

(c) **Income.** A very small proportion of the Bank's funds come from the Bank's earnings.

As it developed, the World Bank turned its attention from Europe to the poorer countries of the world. Today it is almost wholly concerned with helping LDCs. Besides making loans, it's a valuable source of advice and information.

The World Bank has also increased its operations by forming new organisations.

(a) The International Finance Corporation (IFC). This was set up in 1956 to enable the Bank to give loans to private companies as well as governments.

(b) The International Development Association (IDA). The object of this organization, set up in 1960, was to make loans for longer periods and on preferential terms to the LDCs. The IDA has become known as the 'soft loan window'.

The IBRD became more outward-looking with the appointment of Robert Macnamara as chairman, but when he was succeeded by A W Clausen this signalled a tougher line towards the Bank by the USA. In recent years the USA has been the more reluctant to give financial support either to the IMF or to the IBRD. Unfortunately there has never been a greater need for their services, with many countries not being able to export enough even to pay the interest on their debts. Under such conditions commercial loans are impossible and aid from international organizations is the only possibility.

The European Monetary System (EMS)

As we have mentioned, the EEC countries attempted to stabilize the value of their own currencies after the Smithsonian agreement. This broke down in the chaotic years of the mid 1970s but was re-established as the EMS in March 1979. All of the members at the time joined except for the UK. The UK government decided that, at a time when exchange rates were highly volatile, it was not in its interest to join. The EMS is based on a hypothetical unit of account called the European currency unit (ECU). (The French, who had a genius for such things, then discovered that an ECU was also an old French coin.) Thus, it is similar to SDRs. The value of one ECU is determined by taking a weighted basket of member currencies. The value of the weight is determined by the relative size of each member's GDP. Table 8.2 gives the weights in 1985. As you can see, sterling is included in the calculation even though it does not belong to the EMS. However, it has subscribed its share of reserves. This is because the UK is a member of the EEC and it is anticipated that she will eventually join. ECUs are also the basis of all EEC dealing and thus for the UK's payments to and from the EEC. You will notice that the newer members currencies (Greece, Portugal and Spain) are not, as yet, included.

Members' currencies are allowed to fluctuate by plus or minus 2¼% of the value of the ECU. (The lira is allowed to fluctuate in value by 6%.)

Table 8.2   European monetary system currency basket

Currency	Amount of currency in basket	Percentage weight in basket
Deutschemark	0·828	37
French franc	1·15	17
Sterling	0·0885	14
Dutch guilder	0·286	11·5
Italian lira	109·0	8
Belgian franc	3·66	8
Luxembourg franc	0·14	0·5
Danish kroner	0·217	3
Irish punt	0·00759	1
		100·0

Bank for International Settlements (BIS)

This institution is based in Basel Switzerland. It was set up after a proposal by the Young Committee in 1930. Its original purpose was to enable central banks to coordinate their international payments and receipts. Originally it arose out of the need to regulate German reparations. It is one of the oldest surviving and most successful of international institutions although the IMF has taken over some of the functions it was originally designed to fulfil.

Since the 1939–45 war, the BIS has acted like a central bank for central banks. The board of the BIS is made up of representatives of the central banks of the UK, France, Germany, Belgium, Italy, Switzerland, Netherlands and Sweden. Other countries such as the USA and Japan also regularly attend meetings.

In addition to promoting the cooperation of central banks the BIS now:
* organizes finance for nations in payments difficulties. Brazil, Yugoslavia and Mexico have all benefited from the BIS's help
* monitors the eurocurrency markets
* provides expert advice for the OECD and the EMS
* runs the EEC's credit scheme

Not only is it one of the oldest surviving international institutions, it is also a self supporting and profit making institution.

Complete brief profiles of as many international institutions as you can. Here are a few to start you off:
— Asian Development Bank (ADB)
— Organisation for Economic Cooperation as Development (OECD)
— General Agreement on Tariffs and Trade (GATT)

Further reading

Prest and Coppock. *The UK Economy* 9th edn. Weidenfeld & Nicolson. Chapter 3.

Crockett, A. *Money: Theory, Policy and Institutions* 2nd edn. Van Nostrand Reinhold (UK). Chapters 15 and 16.

Carter and Partington. *Applied Economics in Banking and Finance.* Oxford University Press. Chapters 12 and 13.

Griffiths and Wall. *Applied Economics.* Longman. Chapter 27.

Cobham, D. *The Economics of International Trade.* Woodhead Faulkner/Lloyds Bank. Chapter 9.

The Economist. *Money and Finance.* Institute of Bankers. Units 4 and 6.

Pratt, M.J. *A Guide to the International Financial System.* Banking Information Service. Chapters 4–7.

Once you feel confident of your knowledge of this topic try to answer the 10 multiple choice questions which follow.

Multiple choice questions

1   Which of the following assets makes up the greatest part of official international reserves:

   a   gold?
   b   foreign exchange (i.e. currencies)?
   c   IMF reserves?
   d   SDRs?

answer

2   In order for a currency to function as a reserve currency it is necessary that:

   a   its value remains stable.
   b   it is freely convertible.
   c   the nation whose currency it is runs a balance of payments deficit.
   d   all of these.

answer

3   For which of the following reasons might a state prefer *not* to keep its reserves in gold:

   a   gold is no longer readily convertible?
   b   its value varies too widely?
   c   very few gold coins are now minted and so consequently are very hard to obtain?
   d   it could gain interest by holding its reserves in other currencies?

answer

4 At the Bretton Woods conference Keynes proposed the creation of a currency termed 'bancor' to be universally accepted unit of account. Since 1947 the most internationally favoured unit of account has been:

a   the dollar.
b   gold.
c   SDRs.
d   the pound sterling.

5 When the Bretton Woods system was set up in 1947 the price of gold was set at:

a   £8.68.
b   £12.50 per oz.
c $38 per oz.
d $350 per oz.

6 The expression 'reserve tranche' refers to:

a   a nation's gold supplies.
b   the first 25% of a nation's IMF quota.
c   fall back reserves held by other countries.
d   the 25% which a nation may borrow from the IMF beyond the amount equivalent to 100% of its quota.

7 The expression 'the snake in the tunnel' refers to:

a   the movement of European currencies such as the deutschemark within the parites established by the EMS.
b   the European currency agreement within the wider parity of the Smithsonian agreement.
c   the fluctuation in sterling price of oil caused by variations in the pound/dollar exchange rate.
d   the divergence between the trade weighted index value of sterling compared with the pound dollar rate.

8 The heavy overseas lending by banks together with problems of bad debts on the domestic market has meant that:

   a a number of banks have collapsed.
   b the profitability of banks has been eroded.
   c capital adequacy ratios have declined.
   d interest rates have remained high.

 *answer*

9 The details of the EMS were worked out by:

   a ministers of the member states.
   b the European Commission.
   c an *ad hoc* committee.
   d the Bank for International Settlements.

 *answer*

10 Which of the following was the chief cause of Mexico's debt crisis in the early 1980s? Was it the:

   a fall in oil prices?
   b rise in oil prices?
   c collapse of the OPEC cartel?
   d rescheduling of debts?

 *answer*

 Answers follow on pages 168–172. Score 2 marks for each correct answer.

Answers

1 The correct answer is **a**.

This may seem surprising and it does depend on how the gold is valued. Provided that you are aware of this we might let you have answer **b** as correct.

International reserves 1982		
	A %	B %
Gold	10.0	55.0
Foreign exchange	81.0	40.0
IMF reserves	5.0	3.0
SDRs	4.0	2.0
	100.0	100.0

The figures in column A give the distribution of international reserves if we keep to the legal fiction of valuing gold at the official price of $35 per oz. However, in column B we have the distribution of gold is valued at market prices. Since the price of gold varies quite a bit so will the distribution.

Needless to say the majority of actual trade is in reserve currencies and not in gold. The amount of official reserves is dwarfed by the size of private currency dealing.

2 The correct answer is **c**.

All of the functions stated in the question are desirable but not necessarily essential. The world's chief reserve currency is the dollar but since 1971 its value has varied from day-to-day so answer **a** cannot be correct. It is usually part of the normal description of a reserve currency that it be freely convertible and yet for many years the pound was a reserve currency but was only freely convertible within the **Sterling Area** (answer **b**). If a currency is to operate as a meaningful reserve currency then obviously there must be enough of it for *other countries* to do business with it and keep reserves in it. For this to happen then there must be a quantity of this currency at large in the world. It must therefore be the case that the nation whose currency it is runs a more or less continuous balance of payments deficit. This was the case with the dollar (and to a lesser extent the pound) in the 1950s and the 1960s. This was done by the USA constantly having large deficits on the capital account of balance of payments. The USA's inability or unwillingness to do this now partly explains the world's difficulties in international liquidity.

If you chose response **d** you were almost right.

3   The correct answer is **d**.

As we saw in question 1 gold is still an important part of international liquidity. Thus, countries still do use it. The question, therefore, is why they might *choose* not to. One major drawback of gold is that it actually costs you money to hold it; that is to say the cost of storing it, guarding it, transporting it etc. Whereas if you hold your reserves in foreign currencies you can conveniently do this by keeping it in, say, Treasury bills of the country concerned, the dollar being favourite for this. So, your reserves accumulate interest while you are holding them. The one major drawback to this is the possibility that the currency in which you are holding reserves may depreciate.

As far as the other answers are concerned:
- **a**: gold is still probably more convertible than most other currencies
- **b**: its value does vary — but then so does the value of most other currencies
- **c**: gold for reserve purposes is usually used in bullion form not in coins.

4   The correct answer is **a**.

The first sentence of the question is meant to mislead you. It is as Alfred Hitchcock would say a McGuffin. Keynes wished to create a hypothetical international unit of account. This being the case, SDRs and ECUs are the nearest equivalent to a *bancor*. However, the most usual unit of account in international trade is the dollar. Look at all the comparisons of incomes, exports, reserves etc., everything is usually denominated in dollars. Therefore, answer **a** is correct. For some years after the Second World War the pound fulfilled a similar function (answer **d**) but today we cannot see the West Germans, for example, evaluating their exports in sterling.

5   The correct answer is **a**.

When the IMF was established the reference point for all currencies was that gold was valued at $35 for 1 oz of gold. At this time the dollar/pound exchange rate was £1 = $4.03. Those with pocket calculators will have determined this as answer **a** — £8.68 or in the currency of the time £8 13s 8½d. This was a slight variation on the price of gold in the UK in the Second World war of 168 shillings. The 1947 sterling price of gold only lasted until 1949 when the UK, along with most other countries, devalued its currency against the dollar. In 1949 the rate went down to £1 = $2.80 or £12.50 per oz of gold (answer **b**). Answer **c** gives the Smithsonian parity for gold while answer **d** is precisely ten times the correct answer!

6 The correct answer is **b**.

The word **tranche** is French for slice and has come to be applied to shares of quotas in international dealings. Under the original arrangements of the IMF, all members were obliged to subscribe their quotas 25% in gold and 75% in their own currency. Nowadays the 25% gold slice has been replaced by a 25% in reserve currencies and SDRs. What was originally known as the gold tranche it is now known as the reserve tranche.

When it comes to borrowing from the IMF a member can borrow the equivalent of its reserve tranche automatically.

7 The correct answer is **b**.

When the IMF system began to disintegrate in August 1971 an attempt was made to patch it up. This gave rise to the Smithsonian agreement of December 1971. Instead of the 1% variation allowed under the IMF rules, currencies were to be allowed to fluctuate by 2¼% either side of the parity. Hence it would be possible for two currencies to diverge in value up to 4½%. However, when the cross parities between 3 countries were considered this divergence could be doubled i.e. up to 9%. The EEC countries decided that this was too much and established their own currency arrangement which only allowed one currency to vary against another by 1⅛%. This therefore gave a maximum possible cross parity variation of 4½% — the EEC members had established their own smaller variation within the larger variation allowed by the Smithsonian Agreement. This became known as 'the snake in the tunnel'. The Smithsonian being the tunnel while the EEC agreement was the snake. The Smithsonian Agreement has long since disappeared and, although the EEC agreement collapsed its successor the EMS is still often referred to as the 'snake'! Those with a taste for the bizarre might like to know that the Benelux countries established an even smaller variation within the snake which was known as the 'worm'!

8 The correct answer is **c**.

A small number of banks in the USA and the UK (e.g. JMB) have collapsed (answer **a**) but this is not specifically connected with overseas lending, although any bank that has collapsed is obviously suffering from bad debts. For most banks recent years have been extremely profitable, so much so that at one time the Chancellor imposed a special windfall profits tax on them. Profits are likely to remain good so long as interest rates remain high. So answer **b** is also wrong. As far as answer **d** is concerned interest rates are not unconnected with overseas lending but the chief reason why they remain so high is the counter-inflationary monetary policies of the Western nations.

Capital adequacy as you will recall from unit 2, is concerned with the relationship between the Bank's equity and long-term loan capital and its total lending. The huge increases in overseas lending in the 1970s and the collapse of many businesses on the domestic market have led to a general decline, worldwide, in capital adequacy. This together with the possibility of default, or rescheduling, is one of the factors placing a brake on new overseas lending.

9 The correct answer is **d**.

This may seem a surprising answer. After all the BIS is located in Switzerland which is not in the EEC. It is a tribute to the standing of the BIS that it was involved in this. The BIS and Switzerland continue to occupy a pivotal role in world finance while not even being in the IMF.

The other answers are quite likely but the question was about the *details* of the scheme. Ultimately the ministers had to approve the scheme (answer **a**) as had the Commission (answer **b**) and there were *ad hoc* committees (answer **c**) but the nuts and bolts were left to the BIS.

10 The correct answer is **a**.

Mexico is a major oil exporting country. During the 1970s when oil prices rose it greatly increased its expenditure and borrowing. Real interest rates were, at the time, relatively low. Mexico became the second greatest debtor nation in the world after Brazil (see MCQ 8, Post-test 8).

The collapse of oil prices in the early 1980s together with the rise of interest rates plunged Mexico into crisis and there was a danger that it would default on its debts. Thus, of the possible options it is **a** which is relevant.

A rise in oil prices would benefit rather than adversely affect Mexico (answer **b**). Answer **a** may look quite likely but Mexico is not a member of OPEC, although doubtless OPEC's inability to control prices has damaged Mexico. So if you chose answer **c** you were almost right.

Answer **d** cannot be correct because the rescheduling of some of its debts was one of the methods by which Mexico avoided default.

Score 2 marks for each correct answer. What was your score? Fill it in on the score grid.

If you scored 12 or less and are still a bit shaky on some points go back and look at the study guide again before proceeding with the post-test any further.

If you are sure you really understand and are familiar with this topic now, try the 10 further questions which are on pages 208–210. Alternatively you can go on to your next topic and do all the post-tests together at the end.

Topic 9   Eurocurrencies

Study guide

We are devoting the last topic of this study guide to the eurocurrency,
markets as does the syllabus. It is a relatively brief topic and one which
is reasonably easy to come to grips with. Dealings in the various markets
are much like those we find in the domestic markets. The key
differences are:

— Dealings are in eurocurrencies
— It is a wholesale rather than a retail market — people do not walk
    into a high street bank to make a eurocurrency deposit. However,
    there is nothing to prevent anyone from doing this, indeed many
    of the participants in the market are individuals even if very rich
    ones
— There is little effective control over the market
— All business is, by definition, international

Now study Figure 9.1 which summarizes the most important features of
the eurocurrency markets. When you go into the exam you should be
able to write about each of the bubbles in the diagram. One feature
which you can see indicated in the diagram is that the dealings in
eurodollars dwarf the dealings in all other eurocurrencies.

Defining a eurocurrency

**A eurocurrency is any deposit in a financial institution which is
not denominated in the national currency.**

For example, deposits of sterling in a French bank which continue to be
counted as sterling and not as francs, are eurocurrency — in this case
eurosterling. A glance at the balance sheet of any commercial bank will
show just how much such business they do. Most eurocurrency deposits
are in dollars.

Most holders of eurocurrency are not nationals of the country
where the deposits are held. For instance, in the example we used
above, few Frenchmen would wish to hold deposits of sterling in
France.

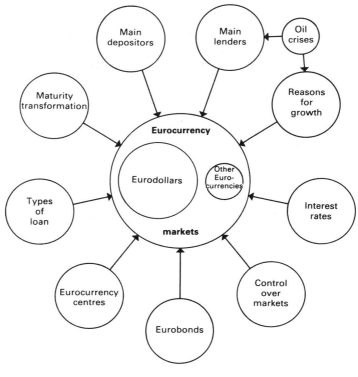

Fig. 9.1

The origins and growth of the markets

The original market was the eurodollar market. This emerged in London in the 1950s to handle the supply of US dollars in Europe. The dollar, you will remember, was then (as now) the most important international unit of account. So companies, not necessarily trading with the USA, demanded dollars for the purposes of international trade.

Up to 1957 sterling also fulfilled a similar role but in 1957 the government restricted its use in third party deals outside the **sterling area**. Merchant banks and others who had specialized in this trade switched to dollars. (Sterling deals in London would not be eurocurrency but dollar deals in London are.) The growth of eurodollars was further accelerated by the growth of dollars in Europe. This was because of:

— US payments *deficits* (See page 159)

— Comecon countries preferring to hold their dollar reserves in London rather than in the USA

— Relaxation of exchange controls in Europe allowed the holding of foreign currency reserves in London by European countries

— Regulation Q which restricted the interest rates which US banks could pay and encouraged Americans to place deposits in London to gain higher rates.

These changes began the process by which London became the world centre of the eurocurrency markets.

The 1960s saw the introduction of new financial instruments into the market such as certificates of deposit. There are now a variety of financial instruments to choose from. The 1960s also saw the beginning of trade in other eurocurrencies, notably the eurodeutschemark. In the 1970s there was a spectacular growth of eurocurrencies. The main reasons for this were:

(a) **The oil crisis.** The huge rise in oil prices in 1973 and again in 1978 left the oil exporting countries with huge dollar surpluses. A very large proportion of these were placed on short-term deposit in Europe.

(b) **Floating exchange rates.** This encouraged speculation and freed many currencies from exchange restrictions.

In recent years (since 1981) the growth of markets has slowed down. This is due to the **world debt crisis.** Up to this date gross lending was growing at 30% per year! The total amount of gross lending is now over £2000 billion. An amount almost equal to the GDP of the USA and *eight times* that of the UK.

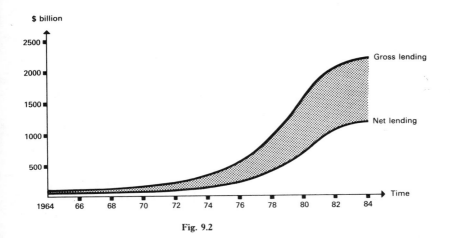

Fig. 9.2

Figure 9.2 shows the growth of eurocurrency lending since 1964. Note the huge growth in the 1970s. The difference between the gross and net figures is that the net figure excludes most inter-bank lending.

As you can gather from these figures, there is much speculative buying and selling. A eurocurrency deposit may change hands several times on its way from ultimate lender to ultimate borrower.

What and where are the eurocurrency markets?

The leading eurocurrency is the dollar, accounting for something like 74% of the market. The second most important is the Deutschemark, other eurocurrencies are the Swiss franc, the yen and sterling. One reason why the pound is a relatively unimportant eurocurrency, while London is the leading market may be obvious to you, i.e. that deals in sterling in London would not be eurocurrency deals. In addition to this, the UK's dealing share in world trade means there is only a limited demand for sterling. A third reason is explained below under the heading of interest rates.

We have just mentioned that the yen is a eurocurrency, we have also seen that the leading currency is the dollar and some of the leading depositors are Arabic. Thus, there is nothing exclusively European about eurocurrencies. This is also reflected in the geographical location of the leading dealing centres. London is the pre-eminent centre. Other centres include Luxembourg, Paris, Canada, Tokyo, Singapore, Hong Kong, Bahrain and Nassau.

Eurocurrency centres are also termed 'offshore markets' (see the previous topic for the definition of these).

Interest rates

The markets would not have grown so rapidly if they did not benefit both depositors and borrowers, i.e. that depositors receive higher interest whilst lenders pay less. How can this be?

Banks can offer higher rates on eurocurrency deposits because the cost of them is cheaper; this stems from the fact that there are no reserve requirements. For instance an American bank is forced to deposit a reserve requirement with the Federal Reserve (central bank) on which it receives no interest but no such requirement attaches to eurocurrency deposits. Thus, a eurodollar is cheaper for a bank to service than a unit of national currency. The bank is therefore able to offer a better rate of interest to the depositor. *For the same reason* it can also charge a borrower at a lower rate. It is thereby working on a lower spread of interest rates. This benefits both borrower and lender.

Much ultimate borrowing has been by less developed countries and has been on a variable rate of interest, usually fixed to LIBOR. The rise in interest rates on eurocurrency markets in recent years has been one of the major causes of distress to debtor nations.

In the last unit we saw that interest rates influenced exchange rates. The reverse is also true. That is to say, an increase in interest rates is likely to cause a currency to appreciate. Eurocurrencies are particularly susceptible to this because they are more volatile.

Maturity transformation

Maturity transformation is an essential part of financial intermediation (see Topic 2). If we examine a bank's balance sheet for its domestic dealing we usually find that it has borrowed money for short periods of time e.g. current accounts, but lent out for considerably longer. However, when we look at a bank's balance sheet in eurocurrency we find that the maturity profile of its lending and borrowing is very similar. This is less so at the long end of the market i.e. loans of 3 years and more.

Note that we are speaking of the *banks* here not the ultimate borrowers and lenders.

Main depositors

In eurocurrency deposits we must distinguish between the ultimate lender and those, like banks, who are essentially redepositing existing deposits. The latter accounts for a lot of eurocurrency dealing.

The main ultimate lenders are:

(a) Oil exporting countries with dollar surpluses. These have become less important in recent years as many of them have swung into deficit as a result of the fall in prices and demand for oil. The only major surplus nations now are Saudia Arabia and the Gulf States.

(b) International companies will deposit money for a number of reasons. First, because they may need foreign currency for trading purposes. Second, to speculate on changes in exchange rate and third, to gain higher rates of interest.

(c) Banks themselves may be ultimate lenders. The main banking participants on the eurocurrency market are American. This helps to explain the presence of so many US (and other overseas banks) in London. In London itself the largest amount of eurocurrency business is done by non-US overseas banks.

Main borrowers

Again there is a distinction between banks borrowing to re-lend and ultimate borrowers. We can list ultimate borrowers as:
* Large commercial companies
* Governments — especially those of less developed countries
* Publicly owned companies, e.g. the Gas Council
* Banks themselves

Types of loans

Eurocurrency loans are mainly short term. Approximately one third of loans are for less than 1 month. This is because the eurocurrency markets cater to a large extent for a short-term currency requirements of banks. In recent years, however, medium-term loans have become more usual and loans of up to 8 years are not uncommon. The banks protect themselves on these longer term loans by:
* Lending at floating rates
* Syndicating loans

Eurobonds

In recent years a eurobond market has developed. Such bonds, issued on behalf of governments or large companies are arranged by a bank which usually arranges a syndicate to float the issue. A secondary market has grown up in trading on these bonds.

One of the chief advantages to the borrower is that the loans are usually at a fixed rate (although variable rate bonds have been issued). The advantage to the lenders is that they acquire a negotiable instrument.

Regulation of eurocurrency markets

Governments try to regulate banks for two main reasons:
* Prudential — to see that the bank does not fail.
* Monetary policy — to affect interest rates or credit for the purpose of directing the domestic economy.

Obviously, international dealings are harder to control but the phenomenal growth of the eurocurrency market has made it important to try to control them because they have impoitant effects on both the domestic and world markets. The collapse of several banks heavily engaged in eurocurrency dealings, e.g. Herstatt (1974) and Banco

Ambrosiano (1982), emphasized the need for prudential control.

In 1975, the Group of Ten established a committee to attempt to supervise international banking. This committee has established the principle of *parental supervision*. This can be explained in the following terms:

(a) When a bank establishes a *branch* overseas its supervision should be the responsibility of the government of the country of the parent bank.

(b) When a bank establishes a fully fledged subsidiary overseas its supervision is to be done both by the parent monetary authorities and those of the 'host' nation.

At the present time control of eurocurrency markets is far from effective. Much concern has been expressed over this. The European Commission, for example, is anxious that the UK should join the EMS as one step towards stabilizing the markets.

Eurocurrency markets and monetary policy

Credit creation can take place in eurocurrency markets as in any other form of financial intermediation. The problem is that this may be beyond the control of national monetary authorities which are trying to restrict growth in the money supply. Thus, such credit creation may contribute to the worldwide problem of inflation.

The extent to which monetary policy can contain or limit the effect of eurocurrency markets on domestic monetary policy depends upon the type of control used. If the authorities use direct control on the *amount* of currency, then these will be an incentive to switch to the eurocurrency markets. For example, in 1979, when the government abolished the 'corset', sterling deposits grew rapidly. This demonstrated that, prior to this, banks had been keeping reserves in eurocurrencies to avoid controls in sterling.

On the other hand, if the authorities use control of interest rates as the method of policy then this will not undermine domestic monetary policies because market forces in the eurocurrency markets will ensure that rates in the euromarkets rise in sympathy with domestic rates. This is because the *arbitrage* between markets would move interest rates together (see comments on interest rate parity theory in the previous topic).

The mobility of eurocurrency deposits is a source of instability bringing unwelcome changes in the exchange rate. For example, if interest rates were raised in the UK this could well lead to a withdrawal of eurodollars and purchase of sterling and hence to an appreciation of the pound or to a growth in the money supply in the UK. Both of these consequences may be unwelcome.

We may conclude that the eurocurrency markets make the operation of monetary policy more difficult.

Further reading

This a difficult topic to read up on in that there is very little in most of the usual textbooks. You are therefore advised to study this topic thoroughly and consult the references mentioned below.

Study Text in Banking. *Monetary Economics*. Brierley, Price Prior. *Unit 11*.

Pratt, M.J. *A Guide to the International Financial System*. Banking Information Service. Chapter 5.

Cobham, D. *The Economics of International Trade*. Woodhead-Faulkner/ Lloyds Bank. Chapter 10.

The Economist. *Money and Finance*. Brief No. 5.

Once you feel confident about your knowledge of this topic try to answer the multiple choice questions which follow.

Multiple choice questions

1 Which of the following is the best description of eurocurrency:

   a a currency held in its original denomination but in another country?

   b any deposit in a financial institution in a foreign country which continues to be denominated in the currency of its country of origin?

   c an American dollar held in a bank or similar financial institution outside the USA which continues to be denominated in dollars?

   d those currencies which like the dollar or the pound are in common usage within the eurocurrency area?

 answer

2 The largest centre for the eurocurrency market in terms of the value of business transacted is:

   a London
   b New York.
   c Zurich.
   d Hong Kong.

 answer

3 Which of the following is a feature of the eurocurrency market? It:

   a leads to an integration of capital markets.
   b hinders the growth of world trade and development because so many of the currency flows are speculative.
   c reduces the supply of short-term funds available to banks.
   d increases the payments imbalances between countries.

 answer

4 Of the following factors, which has the most restricted the growth of the eurocurrency market:

   a the imposition of restrictions on bank deposits and lending in domestic markets?

    b   restrictions of IMF lending?

    c   the fall in oil prices leading to payments deficits in oil exporting countries?

    d   rescheduling of debts of less developed countries?

5   Which of the following factors has most encouraged the growth of eurocurrency deposits:

    a   the relatively low cost of deposits because no reserve requirements are demanded?

    b   the arrival of so many US banks in Europe?

    c   developments in communications worldwide?

    d   surplus funds available in European countries?

6   The volume of business done by banks in the eurocurrency market is huge, frequently being greater than their domestic dealings. The risk of doing this amount of eurocurrency in business is often offset by the fact that:

    a   governments interfere to guarantee most eurocurrency business.

    b   most of the business is with other banks and institutions in the money markets and consequently little risk of default is involved.

    c   collateral is nearly always demanded.

    d   much of the business is with the banks' (etc.) own offices overseas.

7   A key difference between the ordinary liabilities and assets which a bank may hold and those which it holds in eurocurrencies is:

    a   they are mainly with commercial rather than ordinary clients.

    b   they are usually in much larger amounts.

    c   the domestic side of the balance sheet reflects the function of financial intermediation whereas eurocurrency dealings are an example of financial disintermediation.

d   there is little or no maturity transformation with eurocurrency deposits.

 *answer*

8   Nassau (Bahamas) is a leading eurocurrency market. Which of the following is the most likely reason for this:

a   it is in the same time zone as New York.
b   English is the local language.
c   there are lots of banks there.
d   all of these.

 *answer*

9   A eurobond is a bond:

a   issued on the capital market denominated in a currency other than that of the country of issue and offered for sale internationally.
b   issued by a member of the eurocurrency market.
c   issued by an American bank in Europe.
d   denominated in a eurocurrency.

 *answer*

10   A bond which is issued with an increasing rate of interest over time (e.g. 6% for first year, 7% for next year and so on) is known as:

a   indexed stock.
b   a rising coupon issue.
c   deep discounted stock.
d   a variable interest stock.

 *answer*

   Answers follow on pages 184–187. Score 2 marks for each correct answer.

Answers

1 The correct answer is **b**.

Let's start first with a definition of eurocurrency and then look at the other answers. A eurocurrency is a deposit in a bank or similar institution which is denominated in another currency. For example, if dollars are deposited in an English bank but the bank still counts (denominates) them as dollars then they are 'eurodollars'.

Answer **a** may seem OK but it leaves out a vital part of the definition which is that a eurocurrency must be some type of deposit in an institution. For example, a dollar in the pocket of an American tourist in Paris is not a eurodollar.

Answer **c** gives the definition of a euro*dollar* — thus, while it is correct, answer **b** is the better definition of a euro*currency*. Answer **d** is not detailed enough to be a definition of a eurocurrency. Although both the pound and the dollar do act as eurocurrencies they must fulfil the conditions stated in **b** before they become such.

2 The correct answer is **a**.

London is significantly the largest centre of the eurocurrency market followed by Zurich and Hong Kong. You may well ask why New York does not figure in the list. The answer to this is that by far and away the largest eurocurrency is the dollar and since according to the definition an American dollar in America is not a eurocurrency New York disqualifies itself.

3 The correct answer is **a**.

In this question we are concerned with the advantages and disadvantages of the eurocurrency market. One of the chief features of the market is that it brings all international markets together. We are moving towards a truly international capital market. Therefore answer **a** is correct.

While much of the trade in eurocurrencies is speculative, the free availability of liquidity is more likely to help trade than hinder it and therefore **b** is wrong. A glance at a bank's balance sheet will show that it holds lots of eurocurrency. Further examination would show that much of this is short-term deposits and therefore **c** is wrong. The eurocurrency market may well increase the currency flows between countries but there is no reason why it should increase imbalances on the balance of payments and therefore **d** is also wrong.

4   The correct answer is **c**.

It might be better to answer this question in reverse and say that one of the major reasons for the growth of the eurocurrency market was the huge surplus generated by the oil exporting nations in the 1970s. It was the placing of these surpluses with European banks which was one of the main sources of eurocurrency deposits. So when oil prices dropped and most of the oil exporting countries slipped into deficit this was a major factor preventing the market from growing so rapidly.

As far as the other currencies are concerned, restrictions by governments (answer **a**) would restrict growth but the trend has been the reverse, i.e. towards deregulation. Answer **b** is irrelevant to this question. The rescheduling of debts (answer **d**) would certainly be painful to the market but as yet this has not happened to any significant degree.

5   The correct answer is **a**.

This is rather a technical one. Answers **a**, **b** and **c** can all be said to have contributed to the growth of the eurocurrency market. In the case of answer **b** American banks have certainly become established in Europe to get a foothold but this is not necessarily a reason for them going into eurocurrencies. Developments in information technology (answer **c**) have certainly helped eurocurrency dealing — but they have also helped all other types of dealing.

Of the options available **a** is the only one which gives a reason why eurocurrencies should have grown disproportionately to other deposits. The argument is that since no reserve requirements are attached to foreign currency deposits (e.g. the 0.5% of eligible liabilities) banks are encouraged to hold these rather than deposits in their domestic currency.

Option **d** is simply wrong. During the growth of the eurocurrency market Europe has tended to find itself in deficit rather than in surplus.

6   The correct answer is **d**.

Again you need to have a precise knowledge of eurocurrency business to answer this one.

Answer **a** is patently nonsense. Nowhere are eurocurrencies guaranteed by governments. I hope you didn't choose this one. While answer **b** may be true it is no more true that it is about a bank's ordinary dealings in short-term assets and therefore does not specifically apply to eurocurrency deposits. The vast majority of eurocurrency dealing is not concerned with the type of borrowing which requires collateral and thus **c** is also wrong.

For many of the participants in the eurocurrency markets e.g. the clearing banks, business often consists of transferring funds from one country to another within the same organization which involves no risk. This significantly diminishes the quantity of apparently 'risky' business.

7 The correct answer is **d**.

When we looked at the nature of banking business in Topic 2 we stressed the importance of maturity transformation in banking business. You may recall that we summarized this by saying that banks 'borrow short and lend long'. When we come to examine the eurocurrency assets and liabilities of banks we find that these maturity profiles are very similar.

Answer **a** falls down because we did not specify the type of bank. Some banks do nearly all their business with commercial clients (e.g. merchant banks). The same point also disqualifies answer **b**. Most eurocurrency assets are highly specialized and there is no suggestion financial disintermediation is occurring. Disintermediation, you will recall, is where ultimate borrowers and lenders deal directly with each other. Since by definition a eurocurrency is a deposit in a bank, intermediation must be taking place.

8 The correct answer is **d**.

We couldn't resist putting this question in order that we could use a definition from The Economist's *'Money and Finance'*. Nassau is an offshore eurocurrency centre. The Economist defines an offshore centre as 'a place with a lot of foreign banks — and a beach'. (!)

No one is entirely sure why a particular place becomes an offshore banking centre. Certainly the exchange control regime must be favourable but the developments in information technology make one place as accessible as another. When we come to consider Nassau as a centre, the seemingly trivial points mentioned in the question become important. It is the biggest eurocurrency on the western side of the Atlantic and thus to be running parallel in time (answer **a**) with the largest financial centre in the world is an advantage. Because the eurocurrency market is dominated by the dollar English has become the common language. Thus, point **b** is also relevant. Answer **c** is axiomatic, i.e. it wouldn't be a centre if there were not lots of banks there!

9 The correct answer is **a**.

A eurobond is adequately defined in response **a**. Like all types of eurocurrency the essential characteristic is that it is a financial asset in one country which is denominated in the currency of another. When we examine the other possible responses we see that these conditions are not stated:

Answer **b** we are not told that this is in another currency, e.g. Barclays could issue a bond in the UK in £s, this would not be a eurobond.

Answer **c** the same problem is found here e.g. Chase Manhattan (UK) could issue a bond in £s in the UK which would therefore not be a eurobond.

Answer **d** the pound is a eurocurrency but obviously financial assets denominated in £s in the UK are clearly not eurocurrency.

10 The correct answer is **b**.

In recent years various different types of eurobonds have emerged. Answers **a**, **b** and **c** are all types of eurobond whereas **d** is something we made up but it could apply to various bonds. A rising coupon issue is one where, as it says in the question, the rate of interest increases each year. This continues until a specified rate has been reached. The bond then remains at this rate of interest until redemption. This gives the lender greater protection against inflation or rises in interest rates.

An indexed stock (answer **a**) works like other indexed linked financial assets. Although in the case of eurobonds we may find both the principal and the interest indexed. A deep discounted stock (answer **b**) is one which is issued at a large discount on its redemption value. This is unusual since it is usually bills which are discounted not bonds. So far there have been few such issues.

Score 2 marks for each correct answer. What was your score? Fill it in on the score grid.

If you scored 12 or less and are still a bit shaky on some points go back and look at the study guide again before proceeding any further.

If you are sure you really understand and are familiar with this topic now, try the 10 further questions which are on pages 213–215. Alternatively you can go on to your next topic and do all the post-tests together at the end.

Post-tests

Pages 190–215 contain 10 further multiple choice questions for each topic.

Questions

Topic 1   The concept of money

1   In most definitions of the money stock the majority is made up of bank deposits. Of the following attributes of money, which does bank deposits fulfill least well:

   a   acceptability?
   b   homogeneity?
   c   divisibility?
   d   portability?

 _answer_

2   At times of high rates of inflation experience shows that people:

   a   are reluctant to accept money.
   b   will seek for alternatives as a medium of exchange.
   c   continue to accept money.
   d   switch to index-linked financial assets instead of bank deposits.

 _answer_

3   Which of the following has never been index-linked:

   a   National Savings Certificates?
   b   Save-As-You-Earn?
   c   Gilts?
   d   Building Society deposits?

 _answer_

4   In a multi-bank system, with a reserve requirement of 12½%, additional cash deposits of £100,000 are made. What is the maximum amount of additional bank deposits which may be created by this initial deposit:

   a   £87,500?
   b   £100,000?

c £700,000?
d £800,000?

answer

Questions 5 and 6 are based on the following items:

(i)   Private sector non-interest-bearing sterling bank deposits.
(ii)   Private sector interest-bearing sterling sight bank deposits.
(iii) Private sector holdings of retail building society deposits and National Savings Bank ordinary accounts.
(iv)   Private sector holdings of sterling bank CDs.
(v)   Building Society holdings of money market instruments and bank deposits.

5 Which of the above items are included in the M2 measure of the money stock:

a (i) and (iii) only?
b (i), (ii) and (iii) only?
c (i), (ii), (iii) and (iv) only?
d none of these combinations is correct.

answer

6 Which of the above items is included in the PSL2 measure of liquidity:

a (i), (ii) and (iii) only?
b (i), (ii) and (iv) only?
c (i), (ii), (iii) and (iv) only?
d all of the items?

answer

Questions 7–10 are assertion-reason type questions. You must decide whether:

a the first statement is true but the second statement is false
b the first statement is false but the second statement is true
c both statements are true and the second is not the correct explanation of the first
d both statements are true and the second is the correct explanation of the first.

191

The table below explains the options open to you.

	a	b	c	d
First statement (1)	True	False	True	True
Second statement (2)	False	True	True	True
Explanation			1 does not explain 2	1 explains 2

7 *First statement* Luncheon vouchers may be considered as quasi-money.
   Second statement Luncheon vouchers are not a medium of exchange.

 *answer*

8 *First statement* The index-linking of a financial asset links the principal to the rate of inflation.
   Second statement With an index-linked financial asset the lender is guaranteed a yield higher than that on other similar non-index-linked assets.

 *answer*

9 *First statement* Gold is not regarded as money in modern society.
   Second statement The value of gold varies quite widely.

 *answer*

10 *First statement* The Chicago School (monetarist) would regard building society deposits as money.
    Second statement Money is anything which is the temporary abode of purchasing power.

 *answer*

Topic 2   The UK financial system

1   Which of the following is the best description of financial intermediation:

   a   banks accept deposits and lend to customers?
   b   assurance companies accept premiums from policy holders?
   c   ultimate borrowers are linked to ultimate lenders by means of a third party?
   d   banks undertake payments on behalf of their depositors?

answer

2   A liquid asset is a financial asset which:

   a   can quickly be turned into cash with little or no loss.
   b   is acceptable to the Bank of England as part of a bank's reserve requirement.
   c   is highly volatile.
   d   can readily be used in payment.

answer

3   Which of the following would normally produce the highest yield for a commercial bank:

   a   shares in a non-bank subsidiary?
   b   eurocurrency CDs?
   c   first class bills of exchange?
   d   advances to customers?

answer

4   The optimum size of a bank's balance sheet is the size at which:

   a   the marginal cost of attracting another £1 of deposits is equal to the marginal yield on loans.
   b   it achieves the highest yield from its portfolio of assets.
   c   the net productivity of its capital is maximized.
   d   it achieves the correct portfolio balance.

answer

5 The ratio of capital base to the adjusted total risk assets is known as the:

  a   capital gearing ratio.
  b   free resources ratio.
  c   risk assets ratio.
  d   capital risk ratio.

answer

6 Building societies have proved very popular with savers in recent years because:

  a   they open on Saturdays.
  b   they have many branches.
  c   their shareholders enjoy tax privileges.
  d   they offer a wide variety of services.

answer

7 A consortium bank is one which:

  a   deals mainly in the eurocurrency market.
  b   is owned by a consortium.
  c   is owned by other banks, no bank having a share holding of more than 50% and with at least one shareholder based overseas.
  d   is correspondent with other banks providing a wide variety of business on a European wide basis.

answer

8 A merchant bank is most usually defined as:

  a   a member of the Accepting Houses Committee.
  b   a member of the LDMA.
  c   any institution so defined under the terms of Monetary control-provisions 1981.
  d   an institution carrying out wholesale banking business.

answer

9 Which of the following best describes the money markets:

   a   those institutions and individuals who deal in near money?
   b   the merchant banks and discount houses?
   c   institutions like the Stock Exchange which deal with the wholesaling of money?
   d   members of the Accepting Houses Committee?

 *answer*

10 Which of the following is *not* generally recognized as a 'parallel' money market. Is it the:

   a   Local authorities market?
   b   Eurocurrencies market?
   c   Finance Houses market?
   d   Treasury bill market?

 *answer*

Topic 3   Interest rates

1 If you placed £1000 on deposit with a building society and after 5 years you discovered that the deposit, including interest now amounted to £1400, this would mean that over the 5 years you must have been receiving a rate of interest of:

   a   6%.
   b   7%.
   c   8%.
   d   9%.

 *answer*

2 Which of the following are most likely to be affected by changes in the rate of interest. Those projects which:

   a   are looking for high profits over a short-period?
   b   are long-term public works programmes?
   c   use small amounts of capital because they are labour intensive?
   d   finance their operations by the sale of equities?

 *answer*

3 In recent years interest rates in the USA have been very high because of the:

   a high value of the dollar.
   b lack of faith in the economy of the USA.
   c large overseas debt of the USA.
   d size of the USA's budget deficit.

 answer

4 Other things being equal a rise in the level of interest rates is likely to increase the:

   a demand for money.
   b external value of the pound.
   c size of the national debt.
   d liquidity preference of the community.

 answer

5 Which of the following is not a true rate of interest:

   a LIBOR?
   b Treasury bill rate?
   c base rate?
   d building societies' 7 day share rate?

 answer

6 An increase in the rate of inflation can be expected to:

   a increase interest rates.
   b decrease interest rates.
   c decrease the level of savings.
   d none of the above.

 answer

7 The liquidity preference schedule shows the relationship between:

    a the rate of interest and the demand for money.
    b the stock of money and the rate of interest.
    c liquidity and expectation.
    d the public's desire to hold money and the level of national income.

 *answer*

Read the following passage before answering questions 8–9
The 'real' or non-monetary theory of interest sees the rate of interest being the result of the interaction of the forces of thrift on one hand and the productivity of investment on the other. Keynes, however, was dissatisfied with this theory stating:

> The rate of interest is not the price which brings into equilibrium the demand for resources to invest with the readiness to abstain from present consumption. It is the price which equilibrates the desire to hold cash with the available quantity of cash.

Keynes argued that there were two different types of decision that people made. First they had to decide how much of their income to consume and how much to save; second they had to decide the form in which their savings (both new saving and existing assets) could be held.

8 In the real theory of interest the 'productivity of investment' refers to the:

    a net productivity of capital.
    b choice between investment and saving.
    c governments' investment rate policy.
    d earnings generated by one more unit of investment.

 *answer*

9 Keynes's theory may be termed monetary because he believed that:

    a it explained the rate of interest.
    b it was to do with money and nothing else.
    c real changes in the economy could be brought about as a result of monetary changes.
    d control of the money supply was the essential prerequisite to directing the economy.

 _answer_

10 Keynes differed from the 'real' school of thought on interest rates because he maintained that:

    a people might wish to hold cash as an asset.
    b the rate of interest was unimportant.
    c saving was determined by the rate of interest.
    d the real productivity of investment was unimportant.

 _answer_

Topic 4 Monetary theory

1 If we took £M3 as the measure of the money stock, which of the following would be the approximate value of V (the velocity of circulation):

    a 2.3?
    b 3.4?
    c 4.2?
    d 7.0?

 _answer_

2 Monetarists would argue that an increase in the money stock would:

    a have no effect upon the rate of interest.
    b increase the convenience yield of other assets.
    c give rise to inflation if the economy is at full employment.
    d have no effect upon money incomes.

 _answer_

3 The development of the quantity theory of money is associated with:

   a   Milton Friedman.
   b   Irving Fisher.
   c   Anna Schwarz.
   d   John Kenneth Galbraith.

answer

4 Which of the following actions of monetary policy would *not* cause direct repercussions upon PSBR:

   a   Funding?
   b   Open market sales?
   c   A call for Special Deposits?
   d   Open market purchases?

answer

5 If the Keynesian view of money is that it is a non-interest bearing financial asset which of the following would give the most acceptable definition of the money stock:

   a   M0?
   b   M1?
   c   M2?
   d   PSL2?

answer

6 A shift to the right of the Phillips curve gives rise to the:

   a   decline in inflation in recent years.
   b   long-run Phillips curve.
   c   expectations augmented Phillips curve.
   d   increased effect of high rates of inflation upon the rate of interest.

answer

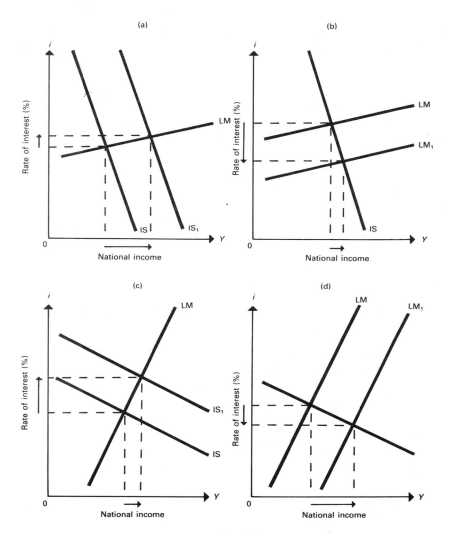

Fig. P-t.1

Questions 7–10 are based on Figure P-t.1. In Figure P-t.1 diagrams **a** and **b** represent a Keynesian view of the economy while **c** and **d** represent the monetarist view. They show the effects of various policy options such as the effects of a budget deficit, the effects of increasing the money supply and so on.

7   Which of the following statements is correct:

   a   a budget deficit brings about a shift to the right in the IS curve and an increase in the rate of interest?

   b   a budget surplus brings about a shift to the left in the IS curve and an increase in national income?

   c   an increase in the money supply would increase the rate of interest and increase the level of national income?

   d   a decrease in the money supply would shift the LM curve rightwards, increase the level of national income and decrease the rate of interest?

answer

8   Of the diagrams in Figure 8 which best illustrates the most beneficial effect of a budget deficit?

answer

9   Of the diagrams in Figure P.1 which best illustrates the greatest effect on the interest rate of a change in the money stock.

answer

10   Of the diagrams in Figure P.1 which best illustrates the greatest effect upon money national income of an increase in the money stock?

answer

Topic 5   Monetary policy

1   Consider the following controls which may be used by the Bank of England. Which one may be described as a qualitative control:

   a   special deposits?
   b   the 'corset'?
   c   a ceiling on banks lending?
   d   a restriction on the percentage of lending to the personal sector?

2   Which of the following weapons of policy available to the Bank of England may be termed a direct control:

   a   open market operations?
   b   funding?
   c   special deposits?
   d   moral suasion?

3   Which of the following was an important modification to the MTFS made in 1985:

   a   M3 was abandoned as a target?
   b   M0 was introduced as a target?
   c   A 'fixed throttle' for monetary expansion was fixed?
   d   PSBR was abandoned as a target?

4   Intermediate policy targets are termed intermediate because they:

   a   are midway to the achievement of final policy goals e.g. reducing the rate of inflation prior to eliminating it.
   b   can only be achieved through the process of financial intermediation.
   c   are medium-term policy objectives.
   d   can be described as neither direct instruments of policy nor final objectives of policy.

5   The Radcliffe Report (1959) stated that there were five objectives of monetary policy. Of the following, which was *not* in that list:

    a   the promotion of economic growth?
    b   assistance to less developed countries?
    c   the redistribution of income?
    d   control of unemployment?

 answer

6   Which of the following would most closely approximate to Friedman's description of 'high powered money':

    a   M0?
    b   Nib M1?
    c   M1?
    d   M2?

 answer

7   Which of the following was not a change introduced in 1981 as part of the Competition and Credit Control (CCC) regulations. Was it the:

    a   introduction of the reserve assets ratio?
    b   introduction of MLR (minimum lending rate)?
    c   abolition of collective setting of interest rates by the clearing banks?
    d   withdrawal of qualitative controls on lending?

 answer

8   The 'corset' (or Special Supplementary Deposit Scheme) differed from other qualitative controls in that it:

    a   acted upon bank's liabilities rather than on their assets.
    b   was discretionary.
    c   only operated from time to time.
    d   was a non-statutory means of control.

 answer

Questions 9 and 10 are based on the following:

The table below represents a simplified balance sheet for Bank X a bank on a multi-bank system. Suppose that the central bank undertakes open market sales.

Deposits	1,000,000	Reserve assets	100,000
		Securities	300,000
		Advances	600,000
	£1,000,000		£1,000,000

£10,000 of these sales are with customers of Bank X. Bank X is obliged to keep a reserve asset ratio of 10%. Assume these open market sales have the greatest possible effect on Bank X.

9   The ultimate level of deposits in Bank X would be:

   a   £2,000,000.
   b   £1,100,000.
   c   £ 900,000
   d   £ 100,000.

 _answer_

10   The amount of reserve assets in Bank X would now be:

   a   £200,000.
   b   £110,000.
   c   £ 90,000.
   d   zero.

 _answer_

Topic 6   Balance of payments

1   In 1984 and for the previous 3 years the UK's largest trading
partner in terms of the total value of imports and exports was:

   a   West Germany.
   b   USA.
   c   France.
   d   Netherlands.

 *answer*

2   Which of the following is the most economically valid reason for
supporting protectionism. It is necessary:

   a   as a defence against 'dumping'?
   b   because tariffs are a valuable source of revenue?
   c   because domestic industry needs to be protected against cheap
foreign labour?
   d   to comply with treaty regulations e.g. EEC import levy?

 *answer*

3   In recent years counter trade has become important to a number of
countries. This refers to:

   a   the direct bartering of goods between countries.
   b   counter cyclical movements of goods and services.
   c   items bought on 'spot' markets, such as oil.
   d   non-tariff forms of protectionism such as imposing special
health and safety requirements on imported goods.

 *answer*

4   Devaluation (or depreciation) of currency is one way in which a
government might attempt to rectify a balance of payments deficit.
However the Marshal-Lerner criterion states that this will only be
successful if:

   a   other countries do not devaluate as well.
   b   it is accompanied by expenditure switching policies such as
import controls.
   c   the demand for exports is elastic.

    d the combined elasticities of demand for imports and exports is greater than unity.

         answer

5 The following figures show the UK's terms of trade for the years 1978–83:

    1978 =   93   1981 = 101
    1979 =   97   1982 = 100
    1980 = 100   1983 = 102

    These figures show:

    a a rise in the price of imports relative to exports.
    b an improvement in the UK's competitiveness.
    c a favourable movement in the terms of trade.
    d an increase in the volume of imports relative to exports.

         answer

6 Of the following reasons which provides the most likely explanation of why a rise in UK real incomes will cause a worsening of the balance of payments situation. The rise in real income will cause:

    a export prices in rise?
    b the volume of imports to increase?
    c an adverse movement in the terms of trade?
    d an increase in the external value of sterling?

         answer

7 The absorption approach to the balance of payments concentrates on the current account. It is based on the Keynesian model of income and we can show the balance as:

$$X - M = Y - (C + I + G)$$

    This implies that:

    a exports and imports are just like other components of national income.
    b imports are absorbed by national expenditure.
    c there is likely to be a payments deficit if total domestic expenditure (TDE) is greater than national income (GDP).

d trade imbalances will have a multiplier effect upon national income.

answer

Questions 8–10 are based on the following information which is the simplified balance of payments accounts of a country (all figures in $m.)

	Year X	*Year Y*
Visible balance	+212	+650
Invisible balance	+800	+1052
Investment and other capital transactions	+659	+987
Balancing item	−351	−289
Foreign currency borrowing (net)	−1200	−1500
Official reserves (drainings on (+) additions to (−))	−120	−900

8 From the above it is possible to determine that:

a official reserves were lower at the end of year Y than at the end of year X.

b exports were greater in year Y than in year X.

c the value of unrecorded items was greater in year X than in year Y.

d the current account balance was more favourable in year Y than X.

answer

9 In year Y the current account balance was:

a +$650m.
b +$1413m.
c +$1702m.
d +$2689m.

answer

10 In year Y the balance for official financing was:

a +£2400m.
b +£2689m.
c −£2400m.
d −£2689m.

answer

Topic 7   Exchange rates

1   It is a weakness of the purchasing power parity theory that:

   a   it is impossible accurately to compare purchasing power
        between nations.
   b   many countries have fixed exchange rates.
   c   many goods and services, the prices of which contribute to the
        calculation of domestic price levels, are not traded.
   d   it attempts to explain the influence of capital movements upon
        exchange rates whereas these are largely independent of
        domestic purchasing power.

 _answer_

2   Which of the following currencies is *not* in the EMS basket of
    currencies:

   a   pound sterling?
   b   deutschemark?
   c   lira?
   d   drachma?

 _answer_

Questions 3 and 4 are based on the following items:
   (i)   ECU.
   (ii)   SDR.
   (iii)   the US dollar.
   (iv)   the pound sterling.
   (v)   the green pound.

3   Which is/are concerned exclusively with EEC transactions:

   a   (i) only?
   b   (i), (iv) and (v) only?
   c   (i) and (iv) only?
   d   (v) only?

 _answer_

4 Which is/are international units of account:

   a (i) and (ii) only?
   b (i), (ii) and (iii) only?
   c (i), (ii), (iii) and (v) only?
   d all of the items?

 *answer*

5 Under the Bretton Woods system the exchange rate regime could be described as:

   a an adjustable peg system.
   b a system of fixed exchange rates.
   c a modified gold standard.
   d Keynesian management.

 *answer*

6 As far as exchange rates are concerned the period from 1947–71 could be described as the era of Bretton Woods. Which of the following do you consider would be the best name for the period since that date, the:

   a era of managed flexibility?
   b OPEC years?
   c age of uncertainty?
   d period of IMF intervention?

 *answer*

7 The decision in 1971 to increase the margins by which currencies could appreciate or depreciate is known as the:

   a Jamaica Conference.
   b Crawling peg.
   c Smithsonian agreement.
   d Snake in the tunnel.

 *answer*

8 In which of the following years was there *not* a major devaluation of sterling:

   a 1931?
   b 1949?
   c 1967?
   d 1971?

 *answer*

9 Which of the following do you consider is likely to provide the greatest obstacle to the return to a regime of fixed exchange rates:

   a lack of reserves of foreign exchange?
   b the difficulty of determining an appropriate rate?
   c lack of a suitable institution to administer such a system after the breakdown of the IMF system?
   d divergences in rates of inflation between different countries?

 *answer*

10 In the UK stabilization of the exchange rate is carried out by the:

   a Exchange Equalisation Account.
   b Bank of England.
   c government.
   d international banks.

 *answer*

Topic 8 International liquidity

1 Gold may not be a satisfactory reserve asset in that it is:

   a very limited in supply.
   b difficult to value accurately.
   c not freely exchangeable.
   d not generally acceptable in payment of debts.

 *answer*

2   Which of the following has not at some time been used for the purposes of international liquidity (or as a reserve asset):

   a the dollar?
   b gold?
   c ECU (European Currency Unit)?
   d silver?

 *answer*

3   When SDRs were created how was their value determined? Was it:

   a the same value as a dollar?
   b based on a basket of 16 currencies?
   c based on a basket of 5 currencies?
   d none of these?

 *answer*

4   Which of the following countries did not take part in the Bretton Woods Conference:

   a Canada?
   b USSR?
   c Germany?
   d France?

 *answer*

5   The General Agreement to Borrow is also known as the:

   a buffer stock facility.
   b currency swap arrangement.
   c compensatory financing facility.
   d group of ten.

 *answer*

6   The chief method by which the surpluses of oil exporting countries were recycled in the 1970s was the:

   a IMF.
   b special supplementary arrangements created by the IMF such as the Oil Facility.

    c   Eurocurrency market.
    d   World Bank.

7   Consider the following selection of foreign currency reserves. Which of these represents the largest proportion of foreign currency reserves:

    a   dollar assets held in the USA?
    b   eurodollar deposits?
    c   other eurocurrency deposits?
    d   claims on countries other than the USA?

8   Consider the following information for the year 1980:

Country	Interest payments on external debt (millions of dollars)	Export of goods and services (millions of dollars)
a Algeria	1305	5240
b Morocco	618	2247
c Mexico	3844	12,050
d Brazil	4142	12,182

Based on these figures which country had the greatest debt service ratio?

9   The greatest proportion of the overseas debt of NOEDCs (non-oil exporting developing countries) is owed to:

    a   foreign governments including the USA.
    b   international institutes such as the IMF.
    c   private sector financial institutions.
    d   non-financial private sector organisations such as the large oil companies.

10 Which of the following is the odd one out:

    a IMF?
    b IBRD?
    c IDA?
    d IFC?

 *answer*

Topic 9   Eurocurrencies

1 Which of the following is a Eurocurrency:

    a French reserves of currency held in UK Treasury bills?
    b an American bank's reserves held in a UK subsidiary?
    c American deposits with a UK clearing bank denominated in dollars?
    d the dollar?

 *answer*

2 Which of the following is *not* a major centre of eurocurrency business:

    a London?
    b Bahrain?
    c New York?
    d Nassau?

 *answer*

3 On which of the following dates did most major European currencies become convertible:

    a 1958?
    b 1967?
    c 1971?
    d 1973?

 *answer*

4 Which of the following has the largest debt on the eurocurrency market:

   a Argentina?
   b Brazil?
   c Mexico?
   d South Korea?

5 If we examined the eurocurrency business transacted in the UK we would find that the greatest percentage of business was done by:

   a London clearing banks.
   b US banks in the UK.
   c Japanese banks in the UK.
   d other overseas banks in the UK.

6 If a customer negotiated a longer term eurocurrency loan from a syndicate of banks this is known as a:

   a syndicated loan.
   b consortium loan.
   c interparty agreement.
   d eurocurrency bond.

7 Which of the following have *not* issued eurobonds:

   a IBRD?
   b IMF?
   c NCB?
   d Bank of England?

8 When a eurocurrency loan for a period of, say, up to 5 years is made subject to the condition that the rate of interest is renegotiated every 3 or 6 months this is known as a:

   a roll-over loan.

b   variable interest loan.

c   negotiable mid-term credit.

d   eurocurrency LIBOR denominated deal.

9   In the eurocurrency market a *tranche* issue is one which is:

a   sold in separate portions.

b   issued in line with IMF tranches.

c   sold to various different institutions.

d   sold at a percentage of its par value, the rest being subscribed later.

10   If a stock was issued and placed with financial institutions and it only became operative once a specified interest rate fell below a stated level, this would be known as a:

a   deep discounted stock.

b   droplock issue.

c   indexed stock.

d   triggered stock.

Answers follow on pages 216–217. Score 2 marks for each correct answer.

Answers

Topic 1 The concept of money

1a	2c	3d	4c	5a
6c	7a	8a	9d	10d

Topic 2 UK financial system

1c	2d	3d	4a	5c
6c	7c	8a	9a	10d

Topic 3 Interest rates

1b	2b	3d	4b	5b
6a	7a	8a	9c	10a

Topic 4 Monetary theory

1b	2c	3b	4c	5b
6c	7a	8a	9b	10d

Topic 5 Monetary policy

1d	2c	3a	4d	5c
6d	7b	8a	9c	10c

Topic 6 Balance of payments

1a	2a	3a	4d	5c
6b	7c	8d	9c	10a

Topic 7 Exchange rates

1c	2d	3a	4b	5a
6a	7c	8d	9d	10a

Topic 8   International liquidity

1a	2d	3a	4c*	5d
6c	7a	8d	9c	10a

*It was in 1944. Think about it!

Topic 9   Eurocurrencies

1c	2c	3a	4c	5d
6a	7b	8a	9a	10b

Score Grid

Topic	Score ?/20	Revision campaign					
		Revision order 1–10	Study guide page no.	MCQs page no.	Score ?/20	Post test page no.	Score ?/20
1							
2							
3							
4							
5							
6							
7							
8							
9							
10							